Reading
Deconstruction
Deconstructive
Reading

Reading
Deconstruction
Deconstructive
Reading

G. DOUGLAS ATKINS

THE UNIVERSITY PRESS OF KENTUCKY

ACKNOWLEDGMENTS

The following chapters have been published in earlier forms: chapter 1 in
Semiotic Themes, ed. Richard T. De George, Univ. of Kansas Humanistic
Studies 53 (Lawrence: Univ. of Kansas Publications, 1981); chapter 2 in *College English* 41 (1980); chapter 4 in *Notre Dame English Journal* 13 (1980);
chapter 5 in *Structuralist Review* 2 (1981). All are used by permission of the
original publishers.

Scholarly publisher for the Commonwealth,
serving Bellarmine College, Berea College, Centre
College of Kentucky, Eastern Kentucky University,
The Filson Club, Georgetown College, Kentucky
Historical Society, Kentucky State University,
Morehead State University, Murray State University,
Northern Kentucky University, Transylvania University,
University of Kentucky, University of Louisville,
and Western Kentucky University.

Editorial and Sales Offices: Lexington, Kentucky 40506-0024

Library of Congress Cataloging in Publication Data

Atkins, G. Douglas (George Douglas), 1943-
    Reading deconstruction, deconstructive reading.

    Includes Index.
    1. Deconstruction—Addresses, essays, lectures.
I. Title.
PN98.D43A84   1983   801'.95   83-10308
ISBN 0-8131-1493-4, cloth; -0165-4, paper

For Leslie and Christopher

Contents

Preface

The following essays are in part designed as an introduction to the important and influential philosophical and critical movement known as deconstruction. Indeed, they directly address the frequently stated need for an account of deconstruction that includes deconstructive readings and that thus both shows and tells. The way in which these essays attempt to achieve these aims, moreover, gives them, I hope, some value in their own right; for some are analyses of important but sometimes scanted aspects of deconstruction, its implications, and its major practitioners, and so of perhaps more than introductory interest, whereas other essays employ deconstructive insights and procedures in the reading of certain "primary" texts. Being both on and in deconstruction, both analyzing and exemplifying it, these essays as a group are intended to reflect the both/and nature of deconstruction, which is one of my foci in the discussions that follow.

In describing and analyzing deconstruction, I have tried to be clear and accurate, though not systematic. Systematizing is put in question by deconstruction, and my effort here has been deliberately essayistic, with all that that entails. Even if its opponents claim the contrary, deconstruction neither prevents nor obstructs the quest of intelligibility and truth. It does, however, enable the humbling recognition, shared with the Bible, that whatever truth is attained is not final or absolute.

The readings undertaken here, and the questions asked, are deeply indebted to the labors of other workers in the critical and theoretical vineyards. These workers are named, however inadequately, in the following essays and their notes. I would like here to acknowledge the specific support, criticism, encouragement, and care offered by friends, colleagues, teachers, and students, none of whom bears any responsibility for whatever errors, mistakes in judgment, and infelicities of expression remain: Bruce Bashford, David M. Bergeron, Andrew P. Debicki, Donald Gray, Susan A. Handelman, Geoffrey Hartman, William P. Kelly III, Helen M. Knode, J. Hillis Miller, Christopher P. Ryan, and Joel Weinsheimer. If for some the so-called critical crisis has set "school" against "school" and critic against critic, even colleague against colleague, for me involvement in heady questions of criticism and theory has been productive of relations and friendships, and I am grateful for that. I am also grateful for the support provided through a fellowship from the School of Criticism and Theory at the University of California, Irvine, and its then director, Murray Krieger—indeed, my work was fostered, in the summer of 1978, in the stimulating and friendly atmosphere of "Kamp Krieger," especially through the inspiring teaching of Geoffrey Hartman and extended arguments with Bruce Bashford, most demanding reader and good friend; a grant from the Mellon Foundation through the University of Kansas Center for Humanistic Studies and its director, Richard T. De George; and the University of Kansas for continued support through grants from the General Research Fund. I want to thank too Penny Parker and Pam Loewenstein, expert and gracious processors of words, and Colby H. Kullman, good friend, for help with the proofreading. I owe a continuing debt both to my wife, Jean, and to my parents. I am most grateful for and to the persons named in the dedication, my children: happy dissemination.

Introduction

Inaugurated in America in 1966 by Jacques Derrida's devastating critique of Lévi-Strauss at a Johns Hopkins symposium, deconstruction has become the critical rage (or, depending upon point of view, outrage). Deconstructive efforts regularly appear not only in avant-garde journals like *sub-stance* and theory-oriented publications such as *Diacritics* but also in major scholarly journals, including *PMLA*. At least one journal (*Glyph*) was evidently established to accommodate if not further deconstructive efforts. Deconstructive readings are by no means limited to essays, however, although that form appears particularly congenial to such efforts, suspicious as deconstructionists are of the totality connoted by the idea of the book; indeed, full-scale deconstructive labors are by now so frequent and widespread as to preclude the necessity, or even the possibility, of specific mention. Deconstruction has so gained in favor and notoriety that its effects on the critical scene have become topics of heated debate, not only in *Critical Inquiry* and the *American Scholar,* but also in mass-media publications such as the *New York Times Book Review, Harper's,* and *Newsweek,* as well as on the *Dick Cavett Show.*

This book does not pretend to account for the phenomenal rise of deconstruction, an issue clearly deserving of analysis. It responds to other needs, Part One being an exposition of deconstructive principles and practices. Whether the essays that make up this part of the book are the reasoned and informed exposition necessary, the reader will decide for himself or herself. Certainly deconstructionists have been loathe to provide any such exposition, owing in part perhaps to the slippery, skidding nature of language, which makes it impossible ever to say exactly what one means or to get it right, as well as to the justifiable fear that exposition will both tame (and perhaps reify) deconstruction and so turn a powerful analytical weapon into merely another ready-made method for the interpretation of individual texts. Though I appreciate the hesitancy and understand the fear, I think the risks worth taking, especially since polemicists (mainly negative) have rushed in where the better-informed have feared to tread, often failing to grasp basic points and so unfairly representing deconstructive aims and principles.

Moreover, those obviously knowledgeable of and indeed well versed in deconstruction have tended to slight some of the important implications of the work of Derrida and others, when they have commented on them. In France, and increasingly in England, deconstruction has been analyzed for its political implications, applied indeed to political problems, and related to Marxism (I think of the Derridean interviews in *Positions* and of Terry Eagleton's recent work); in the work of Gayatri Spivak and Michael Ryan, among others, such implications are now being explored in this country.[1] The relation of deconstruction and psychoanalysis is a major issue, of course, and is receiving due attention from Derrida himself as well as from several others both here and abroad.[2] Many other implications remain to be considered, including for ethics and for teaching. In my view, however, some of the most important, perhaps even revolutionary, implications of deconstruction are for theology and religion. The covert dependence of contemporary theory as revealed in Derrida, Lacan, and Hartman, for instance, on theological modes of exegesis is important and requires analysis, despite the "nontheological" pretensions of many deconstructionists. Susan A. Handelman has begun to explore the relation of Derrida, Lacan, and others to biblical exegesis, but her work is marked, as is that of Bernard-Henri Lévy, by an apparent polemic for Judaism.[3] In Part One of the present book, I too devote considerable attention to the parallels of deconstruction and the biblical vision and provide an assessment of the religious quest in Derrida, Hartman, and J. Hillis Miller. Unlike some others, though, I am willing neither to separate Christianity and Hebraism absolutely nor to hope for the complete dehellenizing of Western thought. I do hope that this book will generate response and further explorations, particularly of the relation of deconstruction and Christianity.[4]

I have mentioned the fear, which I share, that deconstruction will become simply another "method" for the interpretation of texts. A rift is presently growing, in fact, among deconstructionists on the matter of its instrumentality, one rather diverse and indeed heterogeneous group accusing especially the "Yale School" of blunting deconstruction as a means of changing the world by focusing on it as a way of reading which always seems to end in an aporia. I contend that deconstruction is nothing if not a way of reading and that reading is what we are constantly engaged in doing. Is everything therefore a text? In any case, as should be clear to anyone familiar with *Of Grammatology,* de Man's *Allegories of Reading,* and Hartman's *Criticism in the Wilderness,* textual interpretation is hermeneutic and not hermetic and need not be a slave to the text, as it is not in the hands of such deconstructionists; instead, it leads always outward to large questions and issues. If we focus intently on the text, it is not so as to know the text as an object but rather so as to look through it. Guided by but not enslaved to it, we can regard the text as a site, as an opening, and as an opportunity.

My aim in Part One being exposition of deconstructive goals and principles and so a defense of deconstruction against mistaken and distorting polemics, the way of reading I practice there is for the most part thematic and traditional (I am well aware of the difficulties and limitations of such a procedure). A significant change appears in Part Two, the shortest and arguably the most important section of the book, which offers a deconstructive reading of two deconstructionist texts.[5] Though the goal remains the establishment of the nature of deconstruction, the means has obviously changed. In reading these texts with the help of the recent work of Paul de Man, some further misconceptions are cleared up. In addition, the reader can watch in these texts the working out—and not just hear a discussion—of the relationship between writing and reading, between critic and text, between master and slave, and between the declaration a text makes and the description it offers up to a properly close reading. By this point we are reading differently, more closely: attending to the story or allegory the text tells, the story of the unresolvable conflict between textual declaration and textual description and so of the wandering of meaning and of the reader's quest of readability and mastery. It emerges that literary texts, born of language, partake of a both/and nature, both preserving and undoing meaning at once, though we try desperately to stop the ceaseless oscillation and reduce the complication, and interimplication, to the either/or thinking that evidently characterizes Western thinking. The temptation to either/or thinking appears in deconstructionists as well as others, and both cannot but succumb, as we learn in "The Story of Error."

Perhaps I can clarify here my argument concerning the both/and nature of deconstruction, as well as expose some typical misconceptions of it, by briefly considering a critic (who is not, incidentally, a deconstructionist) that I do not discuss in "The Story of Error." My turn to a specific text should not be taken as simply gratuitous, for as Geoffrey Hartman puts it in his latest book, in an age that prefers the electronic media to the painstaking work of reading, Derridean deconstruction "saves the text": there is no escaping the detour of texts, from which our knowledge comes.[6]

The text I wish to consider is William E. Cain's "Deconstruction in America: The Recent Literary Criticism of J. Hillis Miller," which pays impressively close attention to this important and influential critic, who, along with Derrida, de Man, Hartman, and Harold Bloom, is said to form the "Yale School."[7] Cain's valuable essay focuses on certain "confusions" in Miller's work and ends with some sweeping charges against deconstruction as it is currently practiced in this country. The inconsistencies and even contradictions Cain points to are undeniably present in Miller's texts, but I am not at all sure that he has correctly read the story they tell.

Cain repeatedly chastizes Miller, and other American deconstructionists, for an allegedly pusillanimous conservatism. Cain thus writes: "For Miller, 'radical' interpretive possibilities are controlled and held in check by his conservative instincts, which preserve what a thoroughgoing deconstruction would threaten to undermine."[8] It seems to me that what Cain calls for in such passages is closer to destruction than to deconstruction.[9] His "thoroughgoing deconstruction" would simply "undermine" whereas deconstruction, far more radically, insists on an undoing/preserving, or both/and, oscillating movement. Deconstruction is thus not a breaking-down of a hierarchical opposition so as to install a "lower" term in the privileged situation of the displaced. Indeed, deconstruction, as practiced by Miller and others, refuses to rest with the replacement of one term of an opposition by the other, which serves merely to perpetuate hierarchization. Unlike Derrideans, however, Cain would precisely replace one term of an opposition or hierarchy with another, thus continuing our usual way of thinking in oppositions. As I argue at some length in the fourth chapter below, Miller himself rejects such either/or thinking (even if, as I point out in "The Story of Error," inevitable lapses occasionally occur). At any rate, an intervention, deconstruction consists of an undoing/preserving that produces ceaseless reversal, reinscription, and oscillation of hierarchical terms. Complications, relations, and interimplications exist, and stubbornly persist, where one desires neatness, simplicity, and separateness.

The important questions and issues that I have merely raised here are developed in "The Story of Error," and they reemerge powerfully in Part Three, which offers deconstructive readings of three so-called primary texts by Dryden, Swift, and Pope. I have, somewhat arbitrarily, chosen these texts from the period I know best. The texts chosen are important ones, and they themselves, in their particularity, dealing with such issues as reading, interpretation, willing, and difference, help justify my choice, if any justification be required. It also happens that, despite the spread of deconstruction, very little work has been done on the English Augustan Age, though the latter part of the century, particularly on the Continent, has benefitted from the attention of Derrida, de Man, and others, the first two focusing on the work of Rousseau and some others. Thus despite William Beatty Warner's recent book on *Clarissa* and de Man's 1978 essay "The Epistemology of Metaphor," dealing in large part with Locke, my three essays may lay some claim to be breaking new ground.[10] Romantic and "pre-Romantic" texts have now been carefully read, and these readings have begun to suggest some new understandings of literary history. What do so-called classical texts know and have to teach us by means of deconstructive readings?

Part Three of this book raises, differently but insistently, at least two questions worthy of particular notice here. One is the relation of Derrida and de Man, and the other is the relation between a traditional close reading of a text and a deconstructive one. As to the first question, Vincent B. Leitch has helpfully treated the difference between two forms of deconstruction, one deriving directly from Derrida, the other being a variation brilliantly practiced by de Man. Leitch writes: "Rhetorical analysis constitutes a narrow and powerful application of difference insofar as it relentlessly reveals the originating differential and discontinuous nature of literary language. Other applications of difference are possible, as Derrida demonstrates in his many philosophical analyses of conceptual hierarchies. . . . Derrida's conceptual analysis is an alternative to rhetorical analysis in the general work of deconstruction."[11] My essays on *Religio Laici, A Tale of a Tub,* and *An Epistle to Dr. Arbuthnot* all show the influence of de Man, each attending closely to the text's rhetoric, or figurative language. But all three also involve conceptual analysis, the first two exploring the implications for certain major concepts of the texts' figurative language and that on *Arbuthnot* focusing on the relation of self to other. If Derrida and de Man are in an uneasy tension in my essays, I hope that tension is healthy and productive. I do not choose decisively between rhetorical, or figurative, analysis and conceptual.

In Part Three of this book I thus take up again the question of the possibility of choice dealt with in "The Story of Error" and suggest some of the ways in which choices are never (apparently) clear-cut, never a simple either/or matter. These essays raise, as I mentioned, at least a second and related question (concerning the relation between a deconstructive—whether conceptual or rhetorical—and a traditional reading), and I should like to focus on that issue in the remaining pages of this introduction. My chapter on *Religio Laici* perhaps raises the question most forcefully. There, by means of close attention to the poem's figurative language, I—in effect—deconstruct a reading I myself produced some years before. What is the relation between this later, rhetorical reading and the "traditional" one against which it is deployed? The answer is not the perhaps obvious negative one, for I hope to have shown in several essays here that differences within mitigate differences between. Any traditional or unequivocal reading is always already bifurcated, divided within, equivocal, and so the difference between it and the deconstructive one is not that of polar opposition. Instead of being on the outside, distinct, and separate, in fact, the deconstructive already lies within the traditional. Or is it the other way around? It appears that the situation resembles that of host and parasite. If the deconstructive reading seems obviously parasitical on an unequivocal or traditional reading, it can also and equally well be claimed that the unequivocal reading "is the parasitical virus which has for millenia been passed from generation to generation in Western culture in its language and in the privileged texts of those languages."[12] If it be asked which of these readings, the traditional or the deconstructive, is prior or is to be preferred, the answer must come that it is impossible to decide. Each requires the other and indeed contains the other within "itself," thus no longer being a simple identity. Though the essay on *Arbuthnot* in particular, stressing the sexuality of language, deconstructs the ideas of unity and identity and of integral selfhood as an isolated, separable entity, related essays reveal the persistent trace of "the other," "The Story of Error" and the analyses of *Religio Laici* and *A Tale of a Tub* showing the impossibility of thinking writing without reading, slave without master, God without man, and vice versa.

There can be, then, no question of jettisoning, or being able to do without, the traditional or unequivocal reading. As Derrida puts it in *Of Grammatology,* though perhaps with insufficient force or emphasis, "[Without] all the instruments of traditional criticism . . . critical production would risk developing in any direction at all and authorize itself to say almost anything."[13] As attractive as the latter anarchy might be to some, it is not deconstruction. Though it has received scant attention from deconstructionists, of no little importance is the precise kind of reading one has in mind in referring to traditional or unequivocal efforts, against which the deconstructive is played. De Man consistently plays his rhetorical or figurative readings off against what he calls "thematic" readings.[14] He is, of course, far from being the only recent critic to wish to go beyond thematic readings, which have become virtually the sine qua non of contemporary criticism; in a number of traditional critics as well, thematic readings have recently come under well-deserved attack, most notably perhaps Richard Levin writing on Renaissance drama.[15] Is there an alternative traditional criticism, against which deconstruction might be played? Does it matter?

I think yes to both questions. To deal with the second first: To say, as has been done, that one can enter the woven fabric, the textile of the text at any point and proceed from there to offer a deconstructive reading is to spatialize the text, make it static, and reduce its essential temporal dimension (about which more directly). Further, to assume that one can enter the text at either any point or any time is merely to repeat in different guise the strategy of the thematic critic, who arbitrarily and willfully chooses a theme, any theme, to pursue. Moreover, that strategy would deconstruct the text, rather than watch the text deconstruct itself. We approach here again the issue of reader-text relations, which I discuss in "The Story of Error" and the chapter on *A Tale of a Tub,* especially: in short, does the reader impose on the text, does the reader subordinate his or her will and desire to those of the text, or is there a battle of wills and willing between text and reader, another both/and situation? We approach too the issue of reader-responsibility, on which I focus in the chapter on Geoffrey Hartman. The point is Derridean as well, and it has been nicely made by Gayatri Chakravorty Spivak. Derrida, she writes, seeks the means of

> locating the text's "navel," as it were, the moment that is undecidable in terms of the text's apparent system of meaning, the moment in the text that seems to transgress its own system of values. The desire for unity and order compels the author and the reader to balance the equation that is the text's system. The deconstructive reader exposes the grammatological structure of the text, that its "origin" and "end" are given over to language in general . . . by locating the moment in the text which harbors the

unbalancing of the equation, the sleight of hand at the
limit of a text which cannot be dismissed simply as a
contradiction.[16]

The navel, *the* moment, *the* sleight of hand—locating such a
point or time exacts a considerable demand on the "traditional" reading, and it implies far more responsibility to the text
than a thematic reading can offer.

Such responsibility to the text I try to provide in my readings
of *Religio Laici, A Tale of a Tub,* and *Arbuthnot* by first
seeking their "navel." This I do with the help of a way of
proceeding recently proposed by Walter A. Davis in *The Act of
Interpretation.* In those chapters I begin, though I do not end,
with Davis's claim that "the task of interpretation is to appre-
hend the purposive principle immanent in the structure of a
literary work which determines the mutual interfunctioning of its
component parts."[17] What Davis calls the purposive principle
may be seen as the text's navel. Though Davis's argument may
smack of New Critical organicism, it is finally different, locating
a text's immanent purposiveness in its "dynamic progression."[18] This focus on the text's temporal movement in a way
parallels a notion shared by speech-act theorists and at least
some reader-response critics that the reader attend to "what
is being done *in* what is being said."[19] Another way of putting
this is to say that in reading we attend to the performative
function of language and the performative act of the text.

Unlike most other ways of reading, which tend to spatialize
texts, deconstruction too traces a temporal movement, expos-
ing the text's instability, the temporal impossibility of signifier
and signified, of literal and figurative, of performative and con-
stative ever to catch up with one another and to coincide. As
Miller says, deconstruction has to do with "the oscillations in
meaning" that result from the figurative nature of language.
Deconstruction thus shares with the position Davis espouses
a focus on textual motion and the desire to locate the text's

navel, its immanent purposiveness, by means of its "dynamic progression." Deconstruction differs from Davis's position in proceeding to undo or unravel the navel that has nevertheless been preserved and so in denying that the text's movement is one. It is at least double.

As my readings of *Religio Laici, A Tale of a Tub,* and *An Epistle to Dr. Arbuthnot* show, texts can be seen as moving dynamically beyond and even against or counter to any purposiveness that can be attributed to their authors, textual description being precisely a deconstruction of declaration. Due attention to the text's immanent purposiveness, its "dynamic progression," thus may lead *both* to the author's apparent purpose as worked out in the text *and* to the deconstruction of that purposiveness by means of the purposiveness of the text's language. The text tells the story of this conflict. But the conflict is not between two completely different positions, there being no way ever to separate one completely from the other. As Miller says in "The Critic and the Host," "The relation is a triangle, not a polar opposition. There is always a third to whom the two are related, something before them or between them . . . across which they meet."[20] This is sometimes called the trace, *differance,* supplementarity, and occasionally God.

PART ONE
Reading Deconstruction

1. The Sign as a Structure of Difference:

Derridean Deconstruction and Some of Its Implications

A major force in contemporary literary criticism is Jacques Derrida. Derrida's star has risen precipitously since his participation in 1966 in a Johns Hopkins University international symposium, where he took structuralism, and particularly Lévi-Strauss, to task and inaugurated deconstructive criticism in America. The following year he published *La Voix et le phénomène: introduction au problème du signe dans la phénoménologie de Husserl, De la grammatologie,* and *L'écriture et la différence,* all of which are now available in English. In 1972 Derrida published three more books: *La dissémination, Positions,* and *Marges de la philosophie;* these too have recently appeared in English translation. His monumental *Glas* appeared in 1974, and he has subsequently published such books as *Epérons: les styles de Nietzsche* and *La carte postale,* the former already available in English translation. That these books and various essays, several available in English, are changing the face of literary criticism in America is readily apparent.

Not surprisingly, deconstruction has come under frequent and determined attack in scholarly journals as well as in the popular media. Among the charges in these attacks are the claims that Derrida and his followers are needlessly obscure and that deconstructive criticism is nihilistic and deeply antithetical to the so-called humanist tradition. Many of these charges stem, in my view, from a misunderstanding of Derrida, whose work is admittedly complex, whose arguments are often convoluted, and whose style is increasingly difficult. In this chapter, I hope to shed some light on Derrideanism and to clear away some of the confusions surrounding the theory that so many regard as threatening and dangerous. Though my effort will be limited, I hope to provide the kind of general introduction and consideration that has too rarely been attempted on Derrida; most discussions in which Derrida figures prominently assume a basic knowledge of his thought or else proceed to offer an alternative without themselves evincing a grounding in that thought. In the chapters following, I shall consider at length some of the implications of Derrideanism and look specifically at some of the major American deconstructionists.

One cannot hope to understand Derrida apart from his undoing/preserving of the concept of the sign central to modern linguistics. Modern linguistics is often said to begin with Ferdinand de Saussure's *Le cours de linguistique générale.* Probably Saussure's most important argument was that no intrinsic relationship obtains between the two parts of the sign, the signifier and the signified. In his own words, "The bond between the signifier and the signified is arbitrary. . . . *the linguistic sign is arbitrary.*"[1] This is due to the differential character of language. Because the sign, phonic as well as graphic, is a structure of difference, signs being made possible through the *differences* between sounds, that which is signified by the signifier is never present in and of itself. As a result, word and thing, sign and meaning can never become one. "In language," Saussure writes, "there are only differences, *without positive terms.*"[2]

Derrida plays constantly with this discovery that the sign marks a place of difference. But whereas Saussure and Saussurean semiology rest with the binary opposition signifier/signified, Derrida puts such terms *sous rature,* that is, "under erasure." He writes a word, crosses it out, and prints both word and deletion, for though the word is inaccurate it is necessary and must remain legible. This idea of *sous rature* is an analogue of the undoing/preserving play that everywhere characterizes, indeed creates, Derridean thought and so distinguishes it from Saussurean.

Derrida's careful analysis of the sign and of the Saussurean idea of difference leads to several important, indeed far-reaching insights. To describe the structure of the sign, which, he sees, is always already marked by both deferring and differing, Derrida coins the term *differance* (both meanings occur in the French verb *différer*). This notion of *differance* Derrida defines, in *Positions,* as "the systematic play of differences, of the traces of differences, of the *spacing* by means of which elements are related to each other. This spacing is the simultaneously active and passive (the *a* of *differance* indicates this indecision as concerns activity and passivity, that which cannot be governed by or distributed between the terms of this opposition) production of the intervals without which the 'full' terms would not signify, would not function."[3] The possibility of the sign, substituting for the thing in a system of differences, thus depends upon deferral, that is, putting off into the future any grasping of the "thing itself." Space as well as time bears in a fundamental way on the concept of difference, for the temporal interval, the deferring into the future of any grasping of the thing, divides irreducibly all spatial presence. In the movement of thought, elements are never fully present because they must always already refer to something other than "themselves"; or, to change perspectives, if perception of objects depends upon perception of their differences, each "present" element *must* refer to an element *other* than "itself."[4]

In the early essay "Differance," included in the volume translated as *Speech and Phenomena,* Derrida writes, indeed, that

> Differance is what makes the movement of signification possible only if each element that is said to be "present," appearing on the stage of presence, is related to something other than itself but retains the mark of a past element and already lets itself be hollowed out by the mark of its relation to a future element. This trace relates no less to what is called the future than to what is called the past, and it constitutes what is called the present by this very relation to what it is not, to what it absolutely is not; that is, not even to a past or future considered as a modified present. In order for it to be, an interval must separate it from what it is not; but the interval that constitutes it in the present must also, and by the same token, divide the present in itself, thus dividing, along with the present, everything that can be conceived on its basis, that is, every being—in particular, for our metaphysical language, the substance or subject.[5]

Whereas, then, Saussure recognizes that meaning derives from the difference between one element and others in the system, Derrida grasps that *differance* works within as well as between elements. As Jeffrey Mehlman has remarked, "Derrida's effort has been to show that the play of difference, which has generally been viewed as exterior to a (spatial or temporal) *present,* is, in fact, always already at work *within* that present as the condition of its possibility."[6]

As is indicated in the passage quoted from "Differance," what opens the possibility of thought is the retention in the "present" of the "trace" of a past element that was never fully present. Gayatri Chakravorty Spivak calls the "trace" "the part played by the radically other within the structure of difference that is the sign" and proceeds to term it "the mark of the absence of a presence, an always already absent present, of the lack at the origin that is the condition of thought and experience."[7] Perhaps Derrida's clearest account of the "trace," *differance,* and their relationship occurs in the following passage in *Of Grammatology:* "Without a retention in the minimal unit of temporal experience, without a trace retaining the other as other in the same, no difference would do its work and no meaning would appear. It is not the question of a constituted difference here, but rather, before all determination of the content, of the *pure* movement, which produces difference. *The (pure) trace is differance.*"

Though the crucial points seem to me to lie in this passage, I shall quote the following sentences since they clarify this idea. The trace

> does not depend on any sensible plenitude, audible or visible, phonic or graphic. It is, on the contrary, the condition of such a plenitude. Although it *does not exist,* although it is never a *being-present* outside of all plenitude, its possibility is by rights anterior to all that one calls sign (signified/signifier, content/expression, etc.), concept or operation, motor or sensory. This differance is therefore not more sensible than intelligible and it permits the articulation of signs among themselves within the same abstract order—a phonic or graphic text for example—or between two orders of expression. It permits the articulation of speech and writing—in the colloquial sense—as it founds the metaphysical opposition between the sensible and the intelligible, then between signifier and signified, expression and content, etc.[8]

In claiming that "without a trace retaining the other as other in the same" difference could not do the work necessary for meaning to appear, Derrida unarguably goes well beyond

Saussure. Indeed, Saussure's own arguments regarding the differential nature of language require Derrida's notion of *differance* as their logical conclusion, for as Alan Bass has written, "Any other alternative, any attempt to save the value of full presence would lead to the postulation of a point of origin not different from itself (an in-different origin), thus destroying the essentially differential quality of language."[9]

Because the structure of the sign is determined by the "trace" or track of that other which is forever absent, the word "sign" must be placed "under erasure." Derrida writes, "the sign is that ill-named thing, the only one that escapes the instituting question of philosophy: 'what is . . .?' "[10] Without, of course, establishing absence in its place, the "trace" destroys the idea of simple presence, the desire of which, Derrida claims, characterizes Western metaphysics. As he says, "Without the possibility of differance, the desire of presence as such would not find its breathing-space. That means by the same token that this desire carries in itself the destiny of its non-satisfaction. Differance produces what it forbids, makes possible the very thing that it makes impossible."[11] The idea of origin, the reader will already have gathered, is similarly destroyed, for origin is always other than "itself," the idea of origin depending upon the production of temporal and spatial difference that must precede any origin. Denied, too, are those other central oppositions of metaphysics: not only truth/error, presence/absence, identity/difference, and speech/writing but also being/nothingness, life/death, nature/culture, mind /matter, soul/body, man/woman, good/evil, master/slave, and literature/criticism (several of these I shall explore in Part Three, below).

It is not enough simply to neutralize these and other oppositions. Derrida insists that there is always "a violent hierarchy. One of the two terms governs the other (axiologically, logically, etc.) or has the upper hand. To deconstruct the opposition, first of all, is to overturn the hierarchy at a given moment."[12] But only first, for another necessary step follows, in which the reversal just effected must be displaced and the apparent winning term placed "under erasure." To reverse the hierarchy, then, only in order to displace the reversal; to unravel in order to reconstitute what is always already inscribed. The "trace" creates this ceaseless undoing/preserving oscillation. The undoing is no more necessary than the preserving, for without the latter another term would be privileged in a new hierarchy, simple opposition being maintained though reversed, and the "trace" ignored. With the "trace," however, as we have seen, a "thing" is not defined by its difference from "another"; differing from "itself," a "trace" of the "other" always already being present, it cannot be simply defined. The point may be illustrated by citing Derrida's 1966 deconstruction of Lévi-Strauss, in which he undoes yet preserves the latter's well-known binary opposition engineer/*bricoleur:* "From the moment that we cease to believe in such an engineer . . . as soon as it is admitted that every finite discourse is bound by a certain *bricolage* . . . the very idea of *bricolage* is menaced and the difference in which it took on its meaning decomposes."[13]

Obviously, as Spivak observes, Derrida is asking us "to change certain habits of mind: . . . the origin is a trace; contradicting logic, we must learn to use and erase our language at the same time."[14] At stake, we may say, is the question of truth, and I want to explore briefly the implications of Derrideanism for truth. In brilliant analyses of Plato in *Dissemination,*[15] Derrida associates writing, the structure of difference marked by the "trace," and so "the disappearance of a present origin of presence, with the Platonic concept of *epekeina tes ousias* (the beyond all presence)." Because Plato posits what cannot be directly viewed (i.e., the sun) as the origin of the visible, Derrida is able to demonstrate that the presence of the thing itself, the unity of referent and signified, is inseparable from the concept of grammatical difference. If the origin of the thing itself is, as Plato asserts, the invisible "beyond" of all presence, the thing itself can obviously never be present. Truth defined as absolute presence, as presence of the *eidos,* thus becomes simultaneously possible and impossible. As the "trace" requires, the thing itself is doubled, true and not-true. This duplicity, born with the "trace," is "what makes truth possible, thereby destroying truth." Contradicting logic, Derrida thus undoes/preserves "truth." [16]

It may be helpful at this point to take up very briefly another crucial—and related—Derridean idea, and that is the notion of the supplement, brilliantly treated in the sections on Rousseau in *Of Grammatology.* The French word *supplément* is like *difference* in having two meanings: it means both an addition and a substitute. Focusing on the supplement in Rousseau's *Confessions,* Derrida reveals a parallel to the work of the "trace" and *differance.* Space does not permit me to describe Derrida's reading in detail; suffice it to say, with Barbara Johnson, that that reading is "indeed nothing less than a revolution in the very logic of meaning." [17] The logic of the supplement, so to speak, complicates such binary oppositions as Rousseau creates between speech and writing. Thus, instead of opposing "A" to "B," as in logic, we see, as Johnson says, the work of supplementarity, by means of which "B" is at once added to "A" and substituted for it. "A" and "B" are neither opposed nor made equivalent; they are not even equivalent to "themselves." Johnson admirably summarizes Derrida's reading of the supplement in Rousseau:

> While Rousseau's explicit intentions are to keep the two senses rigorously distinct—to know when he means "substitute" and when he means "addition"—the shadow presence of the other meaning is always there to undermine the distinction. On the level both of the signified and of the signifier, therefore, it is not possible to pin down the dividing lines between excess and lack, compensation and corruption. The doubleness of the word *supplément* carries the text's signifying possibilities

beyond what could reasonably be attributed to Rousseau's conscious intentions. Derrida's reading shows how Rousseau's text functions *against* its own explicit (metaphysical) assertions, not just by creating ambiguity, but by inscribing a *systematic* "other message" behind or through what is being said.[18]

A text thus differs from "itself," containing both a declaration and a description, and they war with each other.

An important immediate consequence of the never-annulled "trace," of supplementarity, and so of truth/untruth, is the ubiquity of textuality. That "the central signified, the original or transcendental signified" is revealed to be "never absolutely present outside a system of differences . . . extends the domain and the interplay of signification *ad infinitum.*"[19] Bass is thus correct in stating, "Once one has determined the totality of what is as 'having been' made possible by the institution of the trace, 'textuality,' the system of traces, becomes the most global term, encompassing all that is and that which exceeds it."[20] According to Derrida, nothing escapes textuality: there is simply nothing outside textuality, outside "the temporalization of a *lived experience* which is neither *in* the world nor in 'another world' . . . not more *in* time than *in* space, [in which] differences appear among the elements or rather produce them, make them emerge as such and constitute the *texts,* the chains, and the systems of traces."[21] Derrida proposes, in fact, a "double science," a science of textuality. Once we rethink the metaphysical concept of "reality" in "textual" terms (there are no philosophical regulations of truth, the thing itself being a sign and all "facts" being in "fact" interpretations, as Nietzsche argued), we are left with a world of texts, all of which possess a certain "fictive" or "literary" quality.

In this pervasive breakdown of the relationship to truth and reality, literary criticism is not more exempt from textuality than philosophical and scientific works. Whether or not it has always done so, criticism now decides the meaning of a text. Criticism too is a desire of presence. But "meaning" as a privileged term refers to something outside textuality, outside the system of differences: "a text's meaning is the truth that is present 'behind' or 'under' its textual surface that criticism makes fully present by placing it before us."[22] The "trace," of course, makes meaning so conceived, like truth and presence, impossible. To repeat, there is no originating, privileged signified outside the system of differences and so no "meaning."

The deconstructive critic, in practice, tries to avoid the strong ultimate temptation to seek meaning as truth outside or before the work of difference. Such a temptation is inevitable, for we naturally want to resolve contradictions and to break out of the endless chains of substitutions, which "condemn" us to endless interpretation. We desire a haven outside contingency and temporality, which "meaning," "truth," and an originating signified offer. Indeed, the fact of *differance* seems responsible for this situation: it generates the desire to do the impossible, to unify, to locate a reference outside the system of differences that will bestow meaning, "making equal" as Nietzsche puts it (his term is *Gleich machen*). In any case, author and critic share the desire, and the deconstructive critic must be acutely conscious of the desire in both the authors he studies and in himself.

As Spivak writes, "The desire for unity and order compels the author and the reader to balance the equation that is the text's system. The deconstructive reader . . . [seeks] the moment in the text which harbors the unbalancing of the equation, the sleight of hand at the limit of a text which cannot be dismissed simply as a contradiction."[23] The deconstructive critic, therefore, aware of the differential quality of language and recognizing the fact of the "trace," seeks the moment in any text when its duplicity, its dialogical nature, is exposed. Here, as elsewhere, Freud anticipates deconstructive procedure. In *The Interpretation of Dreams,* for example, he suggests that the reader or interpreter should direct his gaze where the subject is *not* in control: "There is often a passage in even the most thoroughly interpreted dream which has to be left obscure. . . . At that point there is a tangle of dream-thoughts which cannot be unravelled and which moreover adds nothing to our knowledge of the content of the dream." Derrida extends this point, modifying it: it *is* the case that such a tangle adds nothing to our knowledge of the content of the dream-text in terms of what it sets up by itself: "If, however, we have nothing vested in the putative identity of the text or dream, that passage is where we can provisionally locate the text's moment of transgressing the laws it apparently sets up for itself, and thus unravel—deconstruct—the very text."[24] The deconstructive critic thus seeks the text's navel, the moment when any text will differ from itself, transgressing its own system of values, becoming undecidable in terms of its apparent system of meaning. "Reading must always," says Derrida, "aim at a certain relationship, unperceived by the writer, between what he commands and what he does not command of the patterns of the language that he uses. This relationship is not a certain quantitative distribution of shadow and light, of weakness and force, but a signifying structure that critical reading should produce."[25] This undoing, made necessary by the "trace," and so by the duplicitous quality of words and texts, must not be confused with the simple locating of a moment of ambiguity or irony that is somehow incorporated into a text's system of (monological) meaning; rather, it is the moment that threatens the collapse of that entire system.

Having discussed some of the important insights and effects of Derrideanism, I wish now to consider major charges levelled at the position. Earlier I mentioned three specific charges brought against Derrida and his followers (obscurity, nihilism, and threatened destruction of humanistic values), and to these I return.

Undeniably, Derrida's work, as well as that of his "disciples," is demanding and difficult. It is also different from the prose we in America and England are accustomed to. I submit, however, that Derrida et al. are not perversely obscure. Part of the problem is that Derrida draws on authors we know hardly at all, notably Nietzsche and Heidegger and, moreover, that he deals with abstract issues alien to the Anglo-American empirical tradition. Another real difficulty lies, I think, in our expectations as readers, for most of us, more influenced by British empiricism than we might care to admit, expect language, and especially literary-critical language, to be a mirror reflecting truly the nature and contents of the "object" being described. Derrida's point, as we have seen, is precisely that writing is never a simple means for the presentation of truth. What this means, in part, is that even criticism and philosophy must be read scrupulously and critically, teased for meaning; they must, in other words, be interpreted and in exactly the same way as poetry, for example. Language always carries the "trace," whether the text in question be poetic, critical, philosophical, psychological, or what have you. Language may be a medium in a ghostly sense (as Geoffrey Hartman puckishly suggests), but it cannot be a medium in the sense of a neutral container of meaning. Derrida and his followers not only advance this argument, but they also frequently, increasingly, express these points in the form in which they write. In *Glas,* for example, Derrida consciously cultivates a *plural* style, à la Nietzsche, as a way of confounding apparent opposites and switching perspectives.

Sometimes linked with the charge of obscurity is the claim that Derrideanism leads to the abandonment of the usual interpretive procedures. This claim, as well as the charges of nihilism and antihumanism, is made by, among others, M. H. Abrams in a response to J. Hillis Miller's review of the former's *Natural Supernaturalism.* Abrams's essay, entitled "The Deconstructive Angel," is perhaps the most influential attack on Derrideanism to date.[26] According to Abrams, deconstructive criticism places even the most arbitrary reading on an equal footing with the most rigorous, for there appears no way of determining right from wrong readings. But Miller, for one, explicitly denies that "all readings are equally valid or of equal value. Some readings are certainly wrong. Of the valid interpretations all have limitations. To reveal one aspect of the work of an author often means ignoring or shading other aspects. Some approaches reach more deeply into the structure of the text than others."[27] In practice deconstructive criticism is certainly not arbitrary or slipshod. A look at such deconstructionists as Miller and de Man will show just how rigorous and exacting such an interpretive procedure can be. The theory itself, with which this practice is interimplicated, insists, despite what Abrams says, on using customary interpretive procedures. Deconstructive criticism goes *with* traditional reading, preserving as well as undoing. According to Spivak, a deconstructive critic first deciphers a text "in the traditional way," and Derrida is even more direct on this point: "[Without] all the instruments of traditional criticism . . . critical production would risk developing in any direction at all and authorize itself to say almost anything. But this indispensable guardrail has always only *protected,* it has never *opened,* a reading."[28] Failing to understand the "trace," Abrams, like other opponents of Derrida, focuses on the undoing side of the undoing/preserving oscillation.

Should deconstruction allow for the creation in a text of simply any meaning the reader or interpreter wished, it would, I think, deserve the epithet "nihilism." I am giving the name "nihilism" to that situation wherein the mind is regarded as the arbiter, even the creator, of all values. According to Miller, in a book written before he knew Derrida, "Nihilism is the nothingness of consciousness when consciousness becomes the foundation of everything."[29] Though Miller himself has recently and helpfully discussed nihilism (arguing that it is parasitically encased in metaphysics), and though I shall return to the issue in treating Miller in chapter 4, I wish here to consider the question of nihilism in Derrida, hoping that we will emerge with a better understanding of his position. I shall focus on nihilism in the sense given above, believing that the results of such an inquiry will at least suggest the way a response would go to other aspects of nihilism.

As my discussion should have suggested, the original and originating differentiation seems to generate the dream of primal and final unity, which is, however, always deferred, never present here and now. We can never "make equal" or get outside the generating system of differences to locate a reference that will bestow order and meaning. There is no Transcendental Signified, we might say, only textuality (and incarnation?). Myth, though, as Herbert N. Schneidau well argues, serves to make us think that totalization and meaningfulness are possible, comforting us with reassurances regarding a "cosmic continuum."[30] But still the gap remains, no matter how hard we try to close it. The humanistic tradition can be described as one attempt at closure, positing a meaningful world.

For Derrida, like Nietzsche before him, this attempt reveals the force of desire and the will to power. Miller writes in his review of Abrams's *Natural Supernaturalism,* the oxymorons of which title express "the force of a desire" for unity: "The reading of a work involves an active intervention on the part of the reader. Each reader takes possession of the work for one reason or another and imposes on it a certain pattern of meaning." Miller goes on to point out that in the third book of *The Will to Power* Nietzsche relates "the existence of innumerable interpretations of a given text to the fact that reading is never the objective identifying of a sense but the importation of meaning into a text which has no meaning 'in itself.' "[31] According to Nietzsche, "Our values are interpreted *into* things"; " 'Interpretation,' the introduction of meaning—not 'explanation' (in most cases a new interpretation over an old interpretation that has become incomprehensible, that is now itself only a sign)";

"Ultimately, man finds in things nothing but what he himself has imported into them"; "In fact, interpretation is itself a means of becoming master of something."[32] Man gives—creates—meaning, then, expressing a will to power as he attempts to improve upon the way things are.

For Nietzsche and Derrida the question is what to do with the recognition that meaning is a construct brought by the "subject," a fiction made by the force of our desire. Subjectivists and at least some hermeneuticists and Bultmannians seem all too ready to accept a situation which appears to privilege the autonomous consciousness, reversing previous hierarchies and installing fiction in the place of truth and reality. Taken only so far, Nietzsche himself may be viewed as agreeing with this sense of the fictionality of things, whereby "believing is seeing" and interpretation is all there is. Clearly, however, Derrida is not nihilistic in the sense defined above, for he insists throughout that consciousness is no origin, no foundation, there being *no* foundation. He undoes the truth/fiction, reality/consciousness polarities but not, with the advocates of the autonomous consciousness, so as to set up the second term in the place of the first. Fiction can no more exist without truth than truth without fiction or presence without absence; they are accomplices, the system of differences and the "trace" making truth (im)possible. By the same token, the subject "in itself," as center, origin, and goal, is no more possible than the object "in itself."

In Derrida, Miller, and others appears a radical understanding of the fictionality of things, which goes beyond nihilism and the autonomous consciousness to a recognition of the doubleness of what is, of the complicity of truth and fiction. Deconstructionists wish to avoid the interpretive mastery or closure that imports *into* texts and the world meaning as transcendent truth or significance, outside the play of difference. Dangers lurk, of course, including the strong possibility that "the desire of deconstruction may itself become a desire to reappropriate the text actively through mastery, to show the text what it 'does not know.' " Even the deconstructive critic forgets that his own text is necessarily self-deconstructed. He assumes that he at least means what he says. Indeed, even if he declares his own vulnerability, his statement occurs in the controlling language of demonstration and reference. The situation is frustrating but humbling—and inescapable—allowing still another glimpse of the vanity of human wishes. Struggling with the desire of deconstruction, Spivak describes the situation as follows:

> a further deconstruction deconstructs the deconstruction, both as the search for a foundation (the critic behaving as if she means what she says in her text), and as the pleasure of the bottomless. The tool for this, as indeed for any deconstruction, is our desire, itself a deconstructive and grammatological structure that forever differs from (we only desire what is not ourselves) and defers (desire is never fulfilled) the text of our selves. Deconstruction can therefore never be a positive science. For we are in a bind, in a "double (read abyssal) bind," Derrida's newest nickname for the schizophrenia of the "sous rature." We *must* do a thing *and* its opposite, and indeed we desire to do both, and so on indefinitely. Deconstruction is a perpetually self-deconstructing movement that is inhabited by differance. No text is ever *fully* deconstructing or deconstructed. Yet the critic provisionally musters the metaphysical resources of criticism and performs what declares itself to be *one* (unitary) act of deconstruction.[33]

Still, deconstruction may disillusion us about mastery as it demonstrates just how precarious our grasp on meaning is. We are and are not masters, therefore no masters. But we must be careful not to fall into the trap of believing in linear progress, supposedly resulting from this enlightenment and demystification. Nor should we pine with a Rousseauistic (and humanist?)

nostalgia for a lost security as to meaning which we never in fact possessed. Rather than with either faith in progress or nostalgia for "lost" presence, Derrida would have us look with "a Nietzschean *affirmation*—the joyous affirmation of the free-play of the world and without truth, without origin, offered to an active interpretation. . . . [This affirmation] plays the game without security." This "interpretation of interpretation," Derrida adds, which "affirms freeplay . . . tries to pass beyond man and humanism, the name man being the name of that being who, through the history of metaphysics or of ontotheology—in other words, through the history of all of his history—has dreamed of full presence, the reassuring foundation, the origin and the end of the game."[34]

For Derrida, as for Schneidau discussing the mythological consciousness, the humanist tradition represents mastery, totalization, closure, nostalgia for a full presence, and the desire of meaning as transcendent truth. The charge that Derrida threatens this tradition is, obviously, valid. Yet, as we have seen, that threat is by no means either nihilistic or simply negative. For many, Derrideanism offers a way through—if not out of—what Schneidau calls "the bankruptcy of the secular-humanist tradition."[35] Indeed, in *Sacred Discontent* Schneidau links Derrida with a very different tradition, the Yahwist-prophetic, arguing that Derrida's work is consonant with the biblical message, which always goes counter to the mythological sense of a "cosmic continuum." Derridean deconstruction, according to Schneidau, is akin to the way in which the Bible insists on the fictionality of things, alienating us from the world, which it empties of "meaning," reminding us constantly of the vanity of human wishes. Yet the Bible's attitude is always ambivalent, at once criticizing and nourishing culture. Schneidau's highly suggestive, and somewhat surprising, argument is far too complex for me to summarize here. A good idea of the nature of that argument, however, may be gleaned from the end of his chapter "In Praise of Alienation," which presents *differance* as far from nihilistic and which sees Derrida as, like the Bible, a positive alternative to mythological and humanist understanding:

> we are [always] open to sudden revelations of meaninglessness or arbitrariness. . . . Sooner or later we are afflicted by the feeling that nothing matters, or "makes any difference," *i.e.,* that we are unable to supply the differentiations which in primitive cultures are articulated by myth, so that our lives and purposes are reduced to entropy. We may flee to various cults, but doubt will have its turn at these. Thus latent Yahwism works within us, leavening all the lump. We are condemned to freedom, not because God is dead but because he is very much alive, as an agent of disillusionment in a basic sense. In this condition, it is not remarkable that we are nihilistic: what is remarkable is that we can become aware of it and acknowledge intermittently the "nothingness of consciousness when consciousness becomes the foundation of everything." So with all self-deceptions: their extent is not as remarkable as our awareness of them. We have reached out for the apple of self-knowledge, and in doing so have alienated God, nature, and each other; but by pressing our self-awareness to its extreme, where we become alienated from ourselves, we find that this is not the end of the story. The Fall is only the beginning of the Bible. To be thus "decentered" (and . . . to be acutely conscious of the fictionality of things) is the precondition of insight: thus it is a *felix culpa,* good news for modern man of a somewhat unlikely kind.[36]

Whether Schneidau is right about the ultimately biblical and Yahwist nature of Derrida's thought is a most important question but beyond the scope of this work to determine. What we can say here is that Schneidau does not come to grips with

Derrida's insistence that *differance* "is not theological, not even in the most negative order of negative theology. The latter . . . always hastens to remind us that, if we deny the predicate of existence to God, it is in order to recognize him as a superior, inconceivable, and ineffable mode of being."[37] For our limited purposes here, whether Schneidau is right or wrong about Derrideanism (despite reservations I, for one, think he is in the main correct) is less important than the possibility he suggests of Derrideanism as an attractive, and positive, alternative to nihilism, the autonomous consciousness, and "the bankruptcy of the secular-humanist tradition."

It may be, as Schneidau suggests, that Derrida offers a long-awaited alternative to certain forms of nihilism. Certainly the challenge he offers cannot be ignored. Since it is unlikely that either benign neglect or wishing will make deconstruction go away, we must come to grips with it, explore its implications, and evaluate it fairly. There are signs that just this kind of thoughtful analysis is under way in religion and theology as well as in criticism and philosophy.[38] Much remains to be done, the work will be difficult, but the prospects are exciting.

2. Dehellenizing Literary Criticism

In a recent essay, entitled "Fear and Trembling at Yale," Gerald Graff lambastes some of today's leading literary critics, principally the "Yale School": Harold Bloom, Paul de Man, Jacques Derrida, Geoffrey Hartman, and J. Hillis Miller. Graff points to the supposed self-absorption of these critics, whose "agony" as critics is said to be the main focus of their criticism; and he remarks on their disjunctive and self-reflexive style, the "creative" response they offer to texts, and their overriding "rejection of objective norms of interpretation."[1] These characteristics, in his interpretation, reflect "modernism weary of itself and knowing it, but not ready to strike out in a different direction."[2] That modernism seems to be epitomized, according to Graff, in Derrida's hope, which I cited in the previous chapter, for a "Nietzschean *affirmation*—the joyous affirmation of the freeplay of the world and without truth, without origin, offered to an active interpretation."[3] Graff writes: "The 'freeplay of the world' is the randomness of a world without intrinsic order or meaning; the 'active' interpretation is that which asserts the critic's freedom in this absurd universe—in contrast to the bad faith of criticism that passively conforms to the text or to its 'origin,' the 'author's intention.'"[4] In the pages that follow, I explore certain aspects of the work of the "Yale School," particularly in light of the charges Graff brings, focusing on Hartman and Derrida. In the next two chapters, I shall be more specific still, devoting a chapter each to Hartman and Miller.

According to Bloom and Hartman, the battle of books implied in Graff's discussion between practical, plainstyle, and "objective" critics and their speculative, visionary, and hermeneutical opponents may be the battle of the Ancients and Moderns all over again.[5] Like Swift's in *A Tale of a Tub,* which engages an earlier battle of books, Graff's faith and that of other plainstyle critics lies in reason, logic, and order—in the classical or Hellenistic view of things. The example of Swift may be instructive. I shall treat *A Tale of a Tub* at some length in chapter 7, but here it may suffice to emphasize that no matter how hard Swift tries in the *Tale,* order and control elude him, the straight line he seeks always curves, and the difference, indeed purity, he hopes for between order and chaos, reason and madness is beyond his grasp: differences stubbornly refuse to be clear, sharp, and total. The satirized Hack speaks truth in spite of Swift when, for example, he observes "how near the frontiers of height and depth border upon each other," adding that "one who travels the east [eventually reaches] the west" and that "a straight line [will ultimately be] drawn by its own length into a circle."[6] Instead of classical unity and identity, the *Tale* reveals inevitable disunity and difference from itself. In spite of his best efforts, then, Swift's text subverts the classical hierarchies. Graff's work could be shown to do the same.

But whether or not order and unity are possible, let alone desirable, these characteristic features of Hellenism are the desiderata for Swift and critics like Graff. Just as clearly, the Yale critics question these and other classical virtues. I do not think, however, that their opposition to the Ancient, classical, Hellenistic view of things can be ascribed to modernism, one feature of which is a "breakthrough" mentality. In fact, the "Yale School" may be seen as opposing modernism as strenuously as Graff (though from a different direction), but they do more than swipe at classicism, a point perhaps to be expected, given that their academic specialties center around the nineteenth century. Their efforts may be seen as directed toward dehellenizing literary criticism, and this is one of their most important shared characteristics.

Hartman has remarked that criticism is the last bastion of neoclassicism, and he may be right. Poetry, the novel, and the drama long ago threw over classicism and its valorization of decorum, linearity, and centering—one has but to think of Sterne, Joyce, and Beckett, among many others. Nietzsche and Heidegger were no less anticlassical, and the same strain appears prominently in twentieth-century theology, as in Reinhold Niebuhr's contention that "the classical culture, elaborated by Plato, Aristotle and the Stoics, is a western and intellectual version of a universal type of ahistorical spirituality."[7]

Hellenism is, of course, inseparable from humanism, and Hartman, for one, believes "we are now nearing the end of . . . Renaissance humanism." In fact, he writes, the feeling among literary critics and scholars for some time has been that "literary humanism was dead." The reason is not hard to find: "given our present sense of the momentum in science, in politics, in the psyche—totalitarian terror, atomic terror, and Freud's hypothesis of an instinctual drive unto death—given all these types of holocaust, it is hard to maintain the humanist's faith in the person: his responsibility, agency, and perfectibility."[8]

Until recently, literary criticism had resisted these surrounding perspectives and pressures. Still, the predominant critical mode, whether expressed by New Critics or historical scholars, remains commonsensical, practical, and "objective." Criticism, as practiced in the twentieth century, decides the meaning of a text. According to one commentator, at least, a text's "meaning" is the truth that, supposedly transcending the play of difference that constitutes language, lies behind or under the textual surface.[9] The belief in stable meaning remains strong, and Graff is certainly not atypical in wishing for "objective norms of interpretation" nor in maintaining the critic's subservience before a master-text, which, as Eliot insisted, he or she is merely to elucidate. For Hartman, such a position is reductive, criticism having more than a functional task. He writes: "To put criticism at a Platonic remove from its object—to consider it as referring to literature without being literary—is to demoralize it as surely as art was demoralized (in theory) by the Platonic notion of its remove from the archetype. Criticism, in short, is not extraliterary, not outside of literature or art looking in: it is a defining and influential part of its subject, a genre with some constant and some changing features."[10] Hartman's anticlassicism is no less apparent when he writes that we should not "make a priori distinctions of a hierarchical kind between the activities of the human mind by freezing them into genres."[11] Yet criticism continues to separate so-called primary and so-called secondary texts in the name of difference, order, and purity. Hartman is clear on the point: "Defensive about their function, [critics] normalize criticism at the price of mystifying creative genius. It is as if the literary field were being crassly divided into permissive creativity (fiction) on the one hand, and schoolmasterly criticism on the other."[12]

In a lively, consciously playful ("I must pun as I must sneeze"[13]), *bricoleur* style, Hartman by his excesses shatters critical—and classical—decorum and thereby the generic and hierarchical distinctions cherished by the classicist. He upsets our expectations of what criticism is to be. Plainstyle criticism, we know after reading Hartman and Derrida, is often precisely that: a silver mediocrity. Isolated from and uncaring about theory and Continental thought with its brooding speculations, compartmentalized and safely removed from politics, philosophy, and theology, and shorn of many intellectual and social tasks, today's critic, at least in America and Britain, seems comfortably ensconced in the Lockean empirical tradition, whether he knows it or not. The style is the man, and the critic's is Gulliverian. No wonder Graff and others are so bothered by the styles of Hartman and Bloom in particular.

Hartman's aniconic style creates the message. His critical style decenters, tests limits, and breaks the clear lines that have been drawn around the critical activity. In his view, criticism must "cross over"—from America and England to the Continent, from literature to philosophy, from the practical to the theoretical, and, perhaps most radically, from "objective" description and elucidation of a master-text to a recognition that criticism too is creative and indeed fictional, differing from the novel, say, in degree but not in kind. The effort is toward demystifying criticism, certainly not purifying it. The possibility of clear, classical distinctions among definite differences is put in question as Hartman valorizes contamination. He writes, for example, that "criticism as commentary *de linea* always crosses the line and changes to one *trans lineam*. The commentator's discourse, that is, cannot be neatly or methodically separated from that of the author: the relation is contaminating and chiastic; source text and secondary, though separable, enter into a mutually supportive, mutually dominating relation."[14] To account for this radical understanding of the collapse of essential differences between literature and philosophy, fiction and criticism, we go to Derrida and his demonstrations that writing *(écriture)* is those texts which reveal their irreducible doubleness. Alan Bass makes the point succinctly: "The 'double science' is . . . the 'science of textuality,' giving a privileged place to what was formerly called 'literature,' but can no longer be called such when the relationship to truth and reality that allegedly distinguished literary, scientific and philosophical texts from each other breaks down as we are forced to rethink the metaphysical concept of 'reality' in terms of textuality. What becomes particularly revelatory for the 'double science' are the ways of reading 'literary' texts that are governed by the classical, metaphysical concepts of interpretation."[15] In the situation thus opened by Derrida, the old distinction between primary and secondary loses meaning, for, as we have seen, *differance* reveals differences within, thereby erasing the radical differences between. Hartman asserts, in fact, that "writing is living in the secondary." He adds, "Things get crossed up in this jittery situation."[16]

In refusing both to reify and to separate genres, disciplines, and distinctions, Hartman rejects the classical sense of unity and totality. Like Derrida, he prefers the term *text* to *book,* for the latter evokes "the idea of a totality, finite or infinite, of the signifier; this totality of the signifier cannot be a totality, unless a totality constituted by the signified preexists it, supervises its inscriptions and its signs, and is independent of it in its ideality. The idea of the book, which always refers to a natural totality, is profoundly alien to the sense of writing. It is the encyclopedic protection of theology and of logocentrism against the disruption of writing, against its aphoristic energy, and . . . against difference in general."[17] Texts thus are open, books closed. It is appropriate that Hartman's last four "books," like most of Derrida's, are collections of individual essays, written over a considerable period of time and (most of them) published separately. One of Derrida's recent "books," *Glas,* which has neither classical beginning nor end and which consists of two columns running simultaneously on each page, continues this decentering, detotalizing activity, advancing it to a new level. The process may also be called dissemination, and it means, to quote Roland Barthes, that "there is never at bottom, in the world, but the writing of a writing: writing sends back always finally to another writing, and the prospect of signs is in a way infinite."[18]

The denial of an Ultimate or Transcendental Signified is perhaps the most important effect of dissemination and *differance.* "Sign" has, of course, always implied the existence of an intelligible "meaning," to which the sign itself refers. What is signified thus becomes a "center" which precedes or follows the sign as a ground. But if, as Saussure argued, signification is determined by the system of differences wherein each sign is inscribed, rather than by the presence of a signified inside and outside language, then it is clear that language has no center. Signifier and signified are both involved in difference. There is no Transcendental Signified, no fullness of presence—only difference. Armed with this powerful insight, Derrida deconstructs logocentrism. That is, he effectively destroys the crowning feature of Hellenism: the idea of the *logos,* the transcendent principle of structure and order that conveys meaning to secondariness. For the "Yale School" there is no *logos* to which an epiphany might lead from an endless chain of texts. In Hartman's words, "Writing is always theft or bricolage of the logos."[19]

These points provide additional insight into the style of the Yale critics, roundly criticized by Graff and others. Their difficult, sometimes opaque styles not only force the reader to think things out for himself, but they also frustrate the drive to transcend the chain of signifiers and reach the signified, to "get the meaning," as if that lay behind the text and governed it. The Yale critics are frequently—and rightly—said to be unclear. What is not sufficiently realized is that the concept of clarity as generally understood may be possible only within the classical conception of the sign, with the signifier on one side, the signified on the other, and the former always in the service of the latter. For the Yale critics, a certain kind of clarity is neither desirable nor possible.

In place of a *logos,* then, a lateral dance. Hartman in *The Fate of Reading* summarizes the situation as follows, acknowledging his own debt to Derrida: "The perpetually self-displacing, decentering movement of the new philosophical style shows that value is not dependent on the idea of some primary or privileged text-moment: value is intrinsically in the domain of the secondary, of *écriture.* Writing is a 'second navigation,' as

Derrida has finely said. With this foregrounding of secondariness I am in agreement."[20]

Is all this a confirmation of Graff's charges that with the "Yale School" we are embroiled in an "absurd universe," where "the 'freeplay of the world' is the randomness of a world without intrinsic order or meaning"? Because the world suggested by the Yale critics *is* one without intrinsic order or meaning, we are no longer in the presence of the Greek *logos*. Derrida's and Hartman's is an anti-Hellenic world.

I mentioned earlier that Hartman regards literary criticism as the last bastion of neoclassicism. It will perhaps surprise many that theology has for some time been "declassicized," "dehellenized." I look now, however briefly, at the dehellenization of theology, for such a consideration will help us understand the project of dehellenizing literary criticism undertaken by the Yale critics.

Though I cannot say when theology began to distinguish Hebraic and Christian thinking from the inevitable Hellenic influence strongly felt in Paul's efforts at accommodation, my reading has uncovered a concerted effort in the 1960s, which is, interestingly, the period when Derrida was beginning to formulate his own attacks on logocentrism (and, as I will suggest, at least some of the Yale critics were already engaged in anti-Hellenic projects). No doubt the theological effort was in part inspired, if not sanctioned, by the well-known work of Paul Tillich, who sought to transcend theism and reach the "God beyond God." To begin with a Roman Catholic example, Leslie Dewart in *The Future of Belief* calls attention to the "progressive dehellenization" of human consciousness and tries to link up theology with that movement.[21] This powerful trend, according to Dewart, effectively spells the end of religion created in the mode of Greek metaphysics, which can discern reality only in *ens,* only in terms of the intelligible and that-which-is. Arguing somewhat like the Anglican John A. T. Robinson in *Honest to God* and Tillich in such works as *The Courage to Be,* Dewart insists that the question is whether God is present, not whether He exists. Among the better-known Protestant anti-Hellenes is Thomas J. J. Altizer, author of, among other books, *The Gospel of Christian Atheism.* Like Dewart, Tillich, and others, Altizer specifically attacks the Christian "bondage to a transcendent, a sovereign, and an impassive God," which derives from the "Greek metaphysical idea of God as an eternal and unmoving Being."[22] Going well beyond Hellenism, Altizer embraces Nietzsche as a guiding spirit and celebrates the very chaos Gerald Graff fears. Altizer writes: "Nietzsche's vision of Eternal Recurrence records the chaos of a world that has fallen away from its original center. It reflects a totality of perpetual and meaningless flux; no longer is there a beginning or an end, or, for that matter, a purpose or goal of any kind."[23] In similar fashion, the Catholic theologian John Dominic Crossan, who has been influenced by Nietzsche, Borges, Barthes, and Derrida, has more recently and joyfully affirmed that "the Holy has no such plan at all and that is what is absolutely incomprehensible to our structuring, planning, ordering human minds."[24] Crossan's various efforts are directed at countering "the classical vision of a fixed center out there somewhere."[25]

The classical vision of a *telos* is connected in these theologians' minds with *hubris.* The Protestant secular theologian Harvey Cox argues, in fact, that teleology reflects a "gnawing mixture of hubris and wishful thinking." He explains, sounding Crossan's note: "It is easy to see an element of *hubris* in teleology. Man experiences himself as a purposeful creature. Unable to believe that the vast cosmos around him is devoid of such purpose, he projects onto it his own purposive style, and sometimes assigns himself a crucial place in the *telos* of the cosmos."[26]

Strange as it may appear to some, these theologians' rejection of the age-old mythological and Hellenic notion of a *telos* and of an order ordained by God and built into the nature of things stems from a recognition that such thinking is unbiblical.

As Herbert N. Schneidau has well argued, "the classical *logos* is none other than the philosophized version of the archaic cosmic continuum"[27]—in other words, a patterned and closed world, which allows man to "found" his existence in the nature of things, thus giving his life meaning and comforting him. The biblical vision, as Schneidau has demonstrated, is radically different. Unsettling to the core, it is open rather than closed and disconfirms rather than affirms structure; an agent of man's disillusion, Yahweh is not to be identified with the idols of the human mind, with nature, place, or structure of any kind: He is known only by displacement, in His acts. He thus seems present only in absence.

The differences between Hellenic and biblical thinking are perhaps clearest with regard to the two understandings of "word." The Greek term *logos* refers to the meaning, the ordered and reasonable content. There is no Hebraic equivalent though *davhar* comes closest to our "word." *Davhar,* however, means not only "word" but also "deed." Borrowing from Thorleif Boman and his authoritative study *Hebrew Thought Compared with Greek,* Harold Bloom has drawn the following contrast:

> *Davhar* is at once "word," "thing" and "act," and its root meaning involves the notion of driving forward something that initially is held-back. This is the word as a moral act, a true word that is at once an object or thing and a deed or act. A word not an act or thing is thus a lie, something that was behind and was not driven forward. In contrast to this dynamic word, the *logos* is an intellectual concept, going back to a root meaning that involves gathering, arranging, putting-into-order. The concept of *davhar* is: speak, act, be. The concept of *logos* is: speak, reckon, think. *Logos* orders and makes reasonable the context of speech, yet in its deepest meaning does not deal with the function of speaking. *Davhar,* in thrusting forward what is

concealed in the self, is concerned with ... getting a
word, a thing, a deed out into the light.[28]

According to Boman, the terms *davhar* and *logos* illustrate
primary and crucial differences between Hebrew and Greek
thought: "on the one side the dynamic, masterful, energetic—
on the other side the ordered, moderate, thought out, calcu-
lated, meaningful, rational."[29] To go a step further, the dyna-
mism of Hebraic thinking results in the genuinely open-ended
nature of the biblical sense of history in contrast to the patterned, closed, and totalized nature of Greek thought. This
distinction in turn reflects the Greek emphasis on space as
opposed to the Hebraic and biblical stress on time. Boman
makes the point while drawing some of its important conse-
quences: "Our notion of eternity inherited from Plato ... is
at base the same thing as the divine beyond ... and is therefore rather more something spatial than something temporal.
The Hebrew language has no word for the same notion; Hebrew equivalents for eternity are temporal to the extent that
they do not signify things beyond but things pertaining to this
life."[30]

I am suggesting what at least some of the Yale critics seem
aware of: their opposition to Hellenism and the classical *logos*
derives from notions strikingly similar to Hebraic and biblical
thought. Indeed, Bloom, who writes that he "prefers the moral-
ity of the Hebrew Bible to that of Homer" and "the Bible aes-
thetically to Homer," remarks in *A Map of Misreading:*
"Though he nowhere says so, it may be that Derrida is substituting *davhar* for *logos,* thus correcting Plato by a Hebraic
equating of the writing-act and the mark-of-articulation with the
word itself."[31] Hartman makes a similar point about Derrida,
observing that he is, in several respects, "Hebrew rather than
Hellene: aniconic yet intensely graphic."[32]

In focusing in the following paragraphs on Derrida's Hebraism, I do not want to minimize the importance in the other critics
of the parallels I have drawn. Nor do I mean to suggest that

Derrida has overly influenced the other Yale critics in this matter. Actually, signs of Hebraism appear variously in Miller's work in the 1960s, and as early as 1954 Hartman was writing in *The Unmediated Vision* about immersion in experience itself at the expense of a transcendent principle; Hartman prophetically concluded, in fact, "The experiment has only started which, clearing the mind for the shock of life, would in time overcome every arbitrary god of the intellect, thus to achieve a perfect induction and a faultless faith."[33] I use Derrida here as a convenient synecdoche.

Derrida's Hebraism is particularly clear in two essays in *Writing and Difference.* "Violence and Metaphysics: An Essay on the Thought of Emmanuel Levinas" begins with a well-known quotation from Matthew Arnold: "Hebraism and Hellenism,—between these two points of influence moves our world. At one time it feels more powerfully the attraction of one of them, at another time of the other; and it ought to be, though it never is, evenly and happily balanced between them." Derrida proceeds to analyze the Hebraic quality of Levinas's thought, particularly in *Totality and Infinity.* Striking Hebraic chords as he writes, Derrida says that Levinas "summons us to a dislocation of the Greek logos, to a dislocation of our identity, and perhaps of identity in general, and to move toward what is no longer a source or a site . . . but toward an *exhalation,* toward a prophetic speech already emitted not only nearer to the source than Plato or the pre-Socratics, but inside the Greek origin, close to the other of the Greek."[34] In the other essay to which I referred, "Edmond Jabès and the Question of the Book," Derrida, following Jabès, aligns writing and Hebraism, affirming "a certain Judaism as the birth and passion of writing"[35] Quoting from Jabès's *Livre des questions,* Derrida adds that "Judaism and writing are but the same waiting, the same hope, the same depletion."[36]

In *Sacred Discontent,* as I suggested in the previous chapter, Schneidau argues that a fundamental congruence exists between Derrida and the Bible. Schneidau demonstrates how

Derrida's attack on logocentrism derives from the biblically inscribed Western tradition of decentering. Derrida is, writes Schneidau, "indebted to the Yahwist vision."[37] The Yahwist vision is stubbornly restless, probing, skeptical, constantly engaged in an effort to demystify and demythologize, attempting to reveal the constructedness and fictionality of all things. As such, that vision is suggested in the *vanitas vanitatum* theme of Ecclesiastes. Whatever its differences from the biblical tradition, the Derridean project bears an obvious similarity to it. The effort, according to John Dominic Crossan, is to overcome "worship of our own imagination" and find a God "who is not our own projected vanity."[38] According to Hartman, we find in Paul de Man such a "religious sense of the vanity of human understanding."[39] An attack on man's pride and on the belief in inevitable progress that will culminate in man's eventual unfolding of all secrets of life is common to the Bible and the Derridean vision. Like Crossan and Miller, I believe, Schneidau finds Derrida a way beyond modern subjectivism, nihilism, and belief in the autonomous consciousness.

Certainly, from the perspective opened up by Schneidau, we can begin to understand Derrida's attack on stable meaning and the Transcendental Signified as like the theologians' impatience with metaphysics. I suppose we can say that with both the point to be questioned and even deconstructed is "isness." If the theologians want to go beyond the God who "is," transcending as it were "the static 'is' as the normative predicate for God,"[40] their aim may not be so different from Derrida's, who denies that we can know anything outside the endless chain of substitutions that are signs. We can know only signs, one pointing to another within the field of substitutions. Even within these sets of relations, nothing is stable because of the "trace." The "trace" establishes difference *within,* meaning that texts of whatever kind are divided, differ from themselves, thus rendering stable and univocal meaning impossible.

In place of stable meaning appears what Derrida calls "free-play," a tremendously creative and exhilarating possibility. The parallel seems close between the conception of freeplay and the dehellenization of theology, which transforms the static idea of God's omnipotence into a sense of the radical openness of history. The result is similar: freedom, notably the freedom to make. "Freed of its sacred aura, the world can now be recreated by man"; it is "totally open to *future creation by man.*"[41] Though the Yale critics would neither sloganize like the theologian nor reify their conceptualizations, Altizer perhaps comes closest to making explicit the parallel I have suggested when he writes: "total affirmation of the world . . . becomes possible only when the world appears as chaos, and man is liberated from every transcendent root and ground."[42]

Such a position can be unsettling, as well as exhilarating. But neither *differance* nor freeplay need arouse the cries of nihilism coming from writers like Graff. Crossan, in fact, has shown how the Bible is dis-seminatively fissured from within, Jesus constantly engaging in freeplay, challenging, even deconstructing the major traditions of Israel's inheritance, as well as those of Christianity. The argument is hardly new, of course, Nietzsche having written in *The Will to Power:* "What did Christ *deny?* Everything that is today called Christian."[43] Whether or not we are ready to hear Nietzsche, we should note Crossan's argument as well as Andrew J. McKenna's account of it in *Diacritics.* McKenna writes that Crossan has articulated "Jesus' opposition to any notion of end and conceivably to any determinate meaning whatsoever. The 'sign of contradiction' fulfills his mission by his playful testimony to the contradiction of signs."[44] McKenna's own contribution, beyond Crossan, is to take with appropriate seriousness Derrida's suggestion in *Glas* to "perfect the resemblance between Dionysus and Christ."[45] McKenna thus returns us to Nietzsche, as do Altizer and Derrida himself: "Jesus' indifference to dogma, etc., partakes for Nietzsche of his active indifference to difference: 'The "glad tidings" are precisely that there are no more opposites'

(*Anti-Christ,* No. 32). It is just this 'faith in opposite values,' which Nietzsche reproaches to metaphysicians."[46]

Despite the similarities I have drawn, on one point at least Derrida appears to differ profoundly from the radical theologians. For he denies over and over again that any such dehellenizing can be complete and total. It is impossible to step outside metaphysics; the attempt to do so will necessarily be couched in the very terms the antimetaphysician aims to dislodge. Thus, despite his claims to the contrary, Lévi-Strauss, for example, remains within the tradition he denies. Derrida insists, therefore, that *differance* "has neither existence nor essence. It belongs to no category of being, present or absent. And yet what is thus denoted as difference is not theological, not even in the most negative order of negative theology. . . . Not only is differance irreducible to every ontological or theological—onto-theological—reappropriation, but it opens up the very space in which onto-theology—philosophy—produces its system and its history."[47] Derrida's rigorous and self-conscious attention to language thus allows for insight beyond the point reached by the theologians.

Moreover, it would be easy enough to show that the oppositions I have repeatedly drawn between Hellenism and Hebraism are neither sharp nor complete. If the theologians, despite their best efforts, cannot ever fully dehellenize theology, the Hellenes themselves can be shown, like Swift, to differ from themselves; in their texts will be found traces of the radically other that in this instance, I have argued, is Hebraism. The point is instructive for literary criticism. It can never be fully dehellenized (or deconstructed) either. Though it can certainly become more self-conscious than at present, it will, must remain impure, both the "Yale School" and the "classical critics" being inextricably involved with one another, bound together in spite of themselves, requiring each other, like host and parasite. In the final analysis, the dehellenizing of literary criticism is as futile as it is inevitable. These points, and many more, the Yale critics are well aware of.

3. Reader-Responsibility Criticism:

The Recent Work of Geoffrey Hartman

Even as reading as an activity has declined, the Age of the Reader has arrived, at least so far as literary theory is concerned. In what amounts to a virtual paradigm shift, emphasis on the reader seems to have replaced focus on "the text itself." Certainly reader-response criticism is now a burgeoning industry, the past couple of years having produced several important books dealing with the reader or the reading process. These include Robert Crosman's *Reading "Paradise Lost,"* William Beatty Warner's *Reading "Clarissa,"* Suzanne Kappeler's *Writing and Reading in Henry James,* Paul de Man's *Allegories of Reading,* Umberto Eco's *The Role of the Reader,* Wolfgang Iser's *The Act of Reading,* Stanley Fish's *Is There a Text in This Class?,* and at least two collections of essays by several hands, *The Reader in the Text,* edited by Susan Suleiman and Inge Crosman, and *Reader-Response Criticism,* edited by Jane P. Tompkins. The last two titles bring together essays representing several theoretical orientations (from New Criticism to structuralism, phenomenology, psychoanalysis, and deconstruction) and in so doing reveal some interesting common ground among competing positions.

As my inclusion of Paul de Man in the list above is meant to suggest, the "Yale School," or "hermeneutical mafia," to which de Man is said to belong, is importantly concerned with the reader and the reading process, even if not directly linked with reader-response criticism as commonly understood. Books by these critics include, in addition to de Man's recent book, Bloom's *A Map of Misreading* and Hartman's *The Fate of Reading,* as well as a host of essays theoretical and critical bearing on reading. Hartman's strong interest in understanding reading continues undiminished in his two most recent books, *Criticism in the Wilderness: The Study of Literature Today* (1980) and *Saving the Text: Literature/Derrida/Philosophy* (1981). In this chapter I want to focus on these important texts, destined, I believe, to make a difference in the way criticism is regarded. I limit my study for both practical and strategic reasons: others have written well on Hartman, and I have treated much of his earlier work in the preceding chapter.[1] I do not mean to imply essential changes in Hartman, but it is particularly his later efforts that have drawn heated remarks from various commentators. I argue that Hartman, who resists the usual labels assigning one to one school or another, now practices and enacts what may be called reader-responsibility criticism (the term is mine, not his), that this differs in important ways from reader-response criticism, and that Hartman's criticism bears close analogies and reveals profound indebtedness to biblical, especially rabbinical, exegesis. I hope that one result of my essay will be to reduce the charges of irresponsibility brought against Hartman and some others, who are frequently said to indulge in "hermeneutical highjinks."[2] The claim bruited about is that the reader is no longer responsible to the text, the (needless) worry that "the reader will be allowed or encouraged to grant his unconstrained subjective responses the status of meaning."[3]

For all the diversity in theoretical orientation that may reside, however uncomfortably, under the umbrella of reader-response criticism, it is clear that such criticism examines "authors' attitudes toward their readers, the kinds of readers various texts seem to imply, the role actual readers play in the determination of literary meaning, the relation of reading conventions to textual interpretation, and the status of the reader's self."[4] Though some such critics (e.g., Gerald Prince) focus on the reader *in* the text, most reader-response critics assume either the reader's dominance *of* the text (e.g., David Bleich and Norman Holland) or the ideal reader's interaction *with* it (Stephen Booth, Stanley Fish, Wolfgang Iser). Especially since Steven J. Mailloux has helpfully detailed the "critical moves" made in reader-response criticism in describing the interaction of reader and text,[5] I shall keep my own description brief. Generally, reader-response critics, including those in the last category just listed, assume a reader who is an active participant in the reading process, not a passive observer. Preferring a temporal rather than a spatial model of the reading experience, these critics are inclined to ask not "what a work *says* or *shows*" but rather "what it *does.*"[6] Meaning, in this view, becomes "an *event,* something that happens, not on the page, where we are accustomed to look for it, but in the interaction between the flow of print (or sound) and the actively mediating consciousness of a reader-hearer." Indeed, "the mind of the reader becomes the 'poem's scene.' "[7] As I have said, variations occur, refinements are necessary in this description, and many questions are raised that I cannot go into here, but the above may serve at least as one context for considering Geoffrey Hartman's reader-responsibility criticism.

In *Criticism in the Wilderness,* moreover, Hartman directly treats aspects of reader-response criticism. For example, he allows us a close glimpse of his response to such criticism when he distinguishes his position from both objective and subjective interpretation. These, he claims, "ignore equally the resistance of art to the meanings it provokes"; whereas objective interpretation "would regulate the understanding, so that it does not waste itself," subjective interpretation "would deregulate it, since the problem is not subjectivity but our overreaction to it, an excess of social rules and psychic defenses" (p. 269). Hartman's alternative (he resists either/or choices), about which more later, is a proposal for indeterminacy, a concept which "explores the 'blind lawfulness' (Kant) of imagination, or how art allows the understanding to produce its own form of meaningfulness" (ibid.). Elsewhere in *Criticism in the Wilderness,* Hartman establishes some distance from what he calls "reader reception," by which he means, first of all, the *Rezeptions-ästhetik* practiced by Hans-Robert Jauss but probably as well the better-known (at least in this country) reader-response criticism of Fish, Iser, and others. "Reader reception," Hartman says, smacks of accommodation: *"of restoring public ability to respond to mythopoeic art"* (p. 88). Suspicious of accommodation and determined to preserve the strangeness and alterity of art, Hartman writes in *Saving the Text* that "critical readers resist the intuitive and accommodating approach, and chart the space between understanding and agreement"; critical reading, he adds, "is not only the reception (*Rezeption*) of a text, but also its conception (*Empfängnis*) through the ear."[8]

At any rate, rather than on the reader, the reading process, or response as these are defined by reader-response critics mentioned above, Hartman stresses, and values, obligation. Instead of response, understood as an emotional or intellectual effect aroused in the process of reading, Hartman emphasizes the reader's engagement, personal involvement, and accountability, the burden and "stress of vocation" that comes with reading. Such a poem as "Leda and the Swan," he writes, "obliges the reader to become active, even to risk something" (*CW,* pp. 272-73). Believing that hermeneutics is "our daily bread," Hartman tries to understand understanding and so is not principally interested in explicating or even understanding a text as a distinct entity. He is more probing and philosophical —more Germanic, if you will—than most reader-response critics. Taken with (and by?) ultimate questions, Hartman finds it impossible, as well as undesirable, to "purify" literature of philosophical or theological "contaminants."

Indeed, Hartman characterizes the critic as one who "relates the adventures of his soul among masterpieces" (*CW*, p. 11). Appearing different from most deconstructionists, including Derrida, whom he certainly admires, Hartman proceeds to claim, like the so-called new hermeneuticists, that in criticism "we deal not with language as such, nor with the philosophy of language, but with how books or habits of reading *penetrate* our lives" (*CW*, p. 203). To the reader, whether critic or not, texts "call" and demand a response. Hartman uses various terms, many of them religious and theological, to describe this situation. He says that "testimony" is solicited, an "answerable style" demanded, as the text "clarifies an existential situation: it places the respondent who accepts the 'point' or 'charge' " (*CW*, pp. 197, 167, 171). A real "burden" falls on the reader or critic, for if "certain works have become authoritative, it is because they at once sustain, and are sustained by, the readers they find" (*CW*, p. 170). In Hartman's view, therefore, a symbiotic relation occurs between texts and readers, each requiring the other: the strength of books, he maintains, "is measured by our response, or not at all" (*CW*, p. 177). Sought by texts is a *strong* response, one that will likely lead to more writing. "The difference that reading makes," Hartman contends, "is, most generally, writing" (*CW*, p. 19). Reading and writing are thus symbiotic also, for "reading at its closest leads to the counter-fabrication of writing. . . . We cannot gain real insight into an artist or ourselves by pure contemplation, only by the contemplation that making (*poesis*) enables" (*CW*, p. 53).

About the kind of response texts demand Hartman is somewhat more specific. The critic's responsibility is, in part, to be patient: to watch and wait in what Hartman, deeply Hebraic, variously describes as a threshold situation and as the wilderness. The great temptation remains to imagine that the Promised Land lies just ahead, with access to it guaranteed by some master theory (*CW,* pp. 130, 165, 185). Such theories offer conclusions and close off "hermeneutical perplexity," and Hartman believes that the negative is the only positive we have. Unlike Matthew Arnold, who thought "our errand in the wilderness would end," Hartman proclaims that "this wilderness is all we have"; even so, "it is better that the wilderness should be the Promised Land, than vice-versa" (*CW,* p. 15). Yet the wilderness needs to be seen as it is and accepted. Commentary's job, accordingly, is "to save the text by continuing it in our consciousness" (*CW,* p. 268), and part of the reader's responsibility is to "keep a poem in mind," for to do so "is to keep it there, not to resolve it into available meanings" (*CW,* p. 274). Hartman insists that major art calls for "exact witness that cannot be co-opted" or merely accommodated (*CW,* p. 183).

The argument for "hermeneutical perplexity" necessarily places a burden on the critical essay, which, says Hartman, "stands at the very intersection of what is perceived to be a past to be carried forward, and a future that must be kept open" (*CW,* p. 199). In *Criticism in the Wilderness,* Hartman devotes considerable attention to the essay, particularly in a previously published chapter entitled "Literary Commentary as Literature." Here he approvingly quotes Pater's contention that the essay is "like that long dialogue with oneself, that dialectic process, which may be coextensive with life. It does in truth little more than clear the ground, or the atmosphere, or the mental tablet" (*CW,* p. 193). Focusing on Lukács's "The Nature and Form of the Essay," Hartman, who elsewhere punningly refers to the usual scholarly article as "the definite article," writes that "in an essayistic mode everything, including the ending, is always arbitrary or ironic: the one question dissolves into the many, and even the external as distinguished from the internal interruptions serve to keep things open. The consciously occasional nature of the essay prevents closure" (ibid.). As a mode of writing, the essay bears an important analogy to the concept of "hermeneutical perplexity," for the essay "acknowledges occasionalism, stays within it, yet removes from accident and contingency that taint of gratuitousness which the mind is always tempted to deny or else to mystify" (p. 194). Linking his discussion of the essay to his own work and specifically to the ideas suggested in his title, as well as to his Hebraism, Hartman writes, "The essayist-critic . . . cannot himself embody the idea. He heralds [Harolds?] it, wakes our sense for it, but remains its precursor . . . the one who foresees but is a threshold figure, like Moses or John the Baptist" (ibid.).

The responsible critic, we may be tempted to conclude from reading Hartman, writes in the essayistic mode, which is probing, open-ended, and inclusive, rather than in the form of the book, which suggests, as Derrida contends, the totality of a system. Accordingly, Hartman says of his own efforts in *Criticism in the Wilderness,* echoing comments quoted above from the discussion of Lukács's essay on the essay: "I am describing a situation, and I have no specific remedy for it. It is only the false remedies, the quack responses, one would be opposing" (p. 157). In a similar vein he declares later, "I want to emphasize the problem rather than pretend to solve it" (p. 211), and at volume's end he writes, "I remain skeptical . . . about the possibility of a truly comprehensive literary theory or literary history" (p. 299). Indeed, one of Hartman's great strengths is his refusal both to systematize and to reduce complex works of art to simple meanings, choices, and responses.

Just as he willingly remains in the wilderness, so he does without some "key" that might open a text or psyche, "slipping 'into all signifying lacunae' like a 'universal phallus' " (*STT,* p. 105). For Hartman, "if there is a key, the author has locked the text and, as it were, thrown the key away—into the text" (ibid.). Perhaps, then, Susan A. Handelman is right when she declares that reading Hartman "one does not feel as when reading Bloom, or de Man, or Derrida that texts are being processed through a pre-determined schema—and roughly forced to yield up their meanings."[9] The name for what Hartman does, I suggest, is reader-responsibility.

Enigmas abound in Hartman's work, his writing resembling that of a *bricoleur,* certainly not an engineer. Quotations ranging from Genesis to Genet and from Boehme to Smart introduce sections of *Saving the Text,* and Hartman alludes to scores of artists literary and graphic, apparently remembering everything he has seen or read. It is obvious that Hartman holds in mind those he treats directly and at some length, such as Lukács, Benjamin, Carlyle, Yeats, and Dickinson (his is not a naively representational view of the critic's function) and that he has been profoundly affected by reading Derrida (still, he can write, for instance: "A restored theory of representation should acknowledge the deconstructionist challenge as necessary and timely, if somewhat self-involved—that is, only occasionally reflective of analogies to its own project in religious writing and especially in literary writing," *STT,* p. 121). Not so obvious, perhaps, are several others whose work bears analogies to Hartman's, work which he does not quite digest—nor mean to digest. Among the more important are Gombrich and his work on the psychology of perception and "the beholder's share"; Jauss and reception-aesthetics; Jean Starobinski's recently translated book which presents Saussure's work on words within words (*Words upon Words*); Bakhtin and his revolutionary sense of the dialogical nature of language; the entire Germanic tradition of hermeneutics, from Dilthey to Bultmann, the "new hermeneutic" of Ebeling and Fuchs, and, of course, both Gadamer and Heidegger; and not least, Martin Buber, whose *I and Thou* is a call to relation, and to whom I shall return shortly. Hartman broods over these and many other texts, "keep[ing] in mind the peculiarity or strangeness of what is studied" (*CW,* p. 26), not fully digesting them (his is also a criticism of indigestion). As he puts it, "The interpreter now evokes the writers of the past in such an engaged and personal way that it is *more* difficult for us to 'digest' or 'assimilate' them" (*CW,* p. 59).

Hartman's own term for his efforts, indebted to Hebraism, a "hermeneutics of indeterminacy," connotes the sense of responsibility I am laboring to describe, for he proposes "a type of analysis that has renounced the ambition to master or demystify its subject" (*CW,* p. 41). Hermeneutics, he insists, "is an art that grows out of perplexity, out of finding an enigma where we expected a kerygma," and indeterminacy as a concept "resists formally the complicity with closure implied by the wish to be understood or the communication-compulsion associated with it." Thus, continues Hartman, "Reading itself becomes the project: we read to understand what is involved in reading as a form of life, rather than to resolve what is read into glossy ideas" (*CW,* pp. 271-72). Distinguishing his interests from typical reader-response criticism, Hartman explains that "indeterminacy does not merely *delay* the determination of meaning, that is, suspend premature judgments and allow greater thoughtfulness. The delay is not heuristic alone, a device to slow the act of reading till we appreciate (I could think here of Stanley Fish) its complexity. The delay is intrinsic: from a certain point of view, it is thoughtfulness itself, Keats's 'negative capability,' a labor that aims not to overcome the negative or indeterminate but to stay within it as long as is necessary" (*CW,* p. 270). Indeterminacy, the essay, hermeneutical perplexity, the wilderness—do not these ideas point to a common concern? Unlike many (most?) other critics, who quest for a key to the Promised Land, Hartman appears remarkably patient in the wilderness—willing to remain "*in the turn* between terms and words" or between words and the Word (*STT,* p. 91).

Indeterminacy also produces contamination, contagion, shuttling, symbiosis, or—to use one of Hartman's favorite words—chiasmus. As he punningly remarks, "end" turns into "and" (*STT*, p. 30), and he suggests the general point when he describes his own activity in the Introduction to *Criticism in the Wilderness:* "I find myself following a personal and maca-ronic procedure in this book. I allow a formal idea within critical theory to elicit the analysis of a poem, and vice-versa; my shuttling between, on the one hand, two critical traditions and, on the other, works of art and works of reading, should be deliberate enough to suggest that criticism is *within* literature" (pp. 5-6). Just as reading cannot be purely separated from writing, or the reader from the text, neither can literature from commentary, literature from philosophy, or even the holy from the profane. Reader and text, for example, simply "cross-over": "criticism as commentary *de linea* always crosses the line and changes to one *trans lineam*. The commentator's dis-course, that is, cannot be neatly or methodically separated from that of the author: the relation is contaminating and chias-tic; source text and secondary text, though separable, enter into a mutually supportive, mutually dominating relation" (*CW,* p. 206). The result? "The situation of the discourse we name *criticism* is, therefore, no different from that of any other. If this recognition implies a reversal," Hartman contends, "then it is the master-servant relation between criticism and creation that is being overturned in favor of what Wordsworth, describing the interaction of nature and mind, called 'mutual domination' or 'interchangeable supremacy' " (*CW,* p. 259).

I have suggested reader-response criticism as a context in which to consider Hartman's differential work on reading and reader-responsibility. Now I would like, more briefly, to suggest some contexts—and with them, philosophical and theological implications—for a more precise understanding of Hartman's call for responsibility. Though I will note some parallels and analogues, I will not mainly be concerned with questions of indebtedness; as I have already indicated, Hartman cannot easily be labeled, he does not subscribe to any "master the-ory," and so we hear in his texts many voices.

We might begin this consideration with Hartman's remark in
Saving the Text on "how much responsibility is on the respondent, on the interpreter. Dialogue itself is at stake" (p. 134). He
explains: "the literary text or artifact is a gift for which the
interpreter must find words, both to recognize the gift, and then
to allow it to create a reciprocating dialogue, one that might
overcome the embarrassment inspired by art's riddling
strength" (pp. 135-36). In other words, troth rather than truth:
"the ability to exchange thoughts in the form of words; to
recognize words of the other; or to trust in the words to be
exchanged. One breaks words with the other as one breaks
bread" (p. 137). Language being dialogical ("the genuine
logos is always a dia-logos," p. 109), relation is required,
and we begin to hear both Bakhtin and Buber. Indeed, Hartman's sense of responsibility bears a close analogy to Buber's
discussion of the centrality of "the unreliable, unsolid, unlast-
ing, unpredictable, dangerous world of relation," from which
man is said to flee in that false drive for "self-affirmation arising
out of the insecurity of life" which often leads to the having of
things.[10] Hartman himself makes the connection in discussing
Bloom's use of Buber in his early book on Shelley: "Like Buber's 'I-Thou,' fundamental words of desire, of an apostrophe
that remains open because the desired 'Thou' is a relation and
not an object and cannot be fixed or imaged except as a
naturalized or neutered 'It,' so an intuition of the discontinuous,
fickle, yet transcendent character of relational bonds saves
Shelley from a belated and superficial allegory of love and a
sentimental worship of past myths" (*CW*, p. 102). Though we
would all prefer (presumably) to have fixed identities and to
keep things "in place," preventing contamination or symbiosis,
crossing occurs, and moreover the text in Hartman's view is a
"Thou," a relation and not an object. The reader's responsibility is to preserve relation and "a reciprocating dialogue."

Because, in Hartman's view, "the genuine logos is always
a dia-logos," writing is "a sort of disaffiliation (a disclosure of

the absence of a single father or unique logos)" (*STT,* p. 121). Hartman borrows Derrida's term for this situation, "dissemination": "that which does not return to the father" (*STT,* p. 48). Indeed, we must abandon "all hope of returning to the father by imitating a Word that was 'in the beginning'"(p. 49), for texts "are so separated from a direct logo-imitative intention by [Derrida's] deconstructive readings that they cannot be returned to the father: their author, or their author in heaven" (p. 51). Words are thus, Hartman argues, scattered and sown, and we must learn "how to reap a page" (the title of the third chapter of *Saving the Text*).

The implications for the reader of the absence of the father and of dissemination are, I take it, somewhat as follows (I draw on Lacan here, as Hartman does): There being no final authority present, no Transcendental Signified, determinate meaning is impossible. Meaning is scattered, dispersed, any "key" having been, as it were, "thrown away—into the text." "This errancy of meaning cannot be gathered back: there is no certain matrix. Language is error and cannot be purified" (*STT,* p. 83). As such major texts as *The Odyssey, Hamlet,* and Joyce's *Ulysses* demonstrate, it is extremely difficult to bear the father's absence, and indeed we usually try to fill the gap by taking the father's place: in this case, positing determinacy where none otherwise exists. Determinate meaning thus becomes a performative act, but such an act is akin to the suitors' usurpation of Odysseus's place in Ithaca and represents self-affirmation and the negation of relation.[11] In terms of reading, it means a willful and egoistic imposition of closure and determinacy, as well as a reductiveness that essentially eliminates "the other." Hartman argues for and enacts, I believe, an alternative via his "hermeneutics of indeterminacy." In the terms I have been using in this essay, with the absence of the father come enormous responsibilities for the reader (were the father simply present, reading would be easy and effortless, consisting of obedience to directions). The reader must act *for,* not *as,* the absent father, not take his place but accept difference from him. The reader must, in short, carry on the work of the absent father, reaping the page that has been sown and left to grow, bearing the responsibility of work.

Indeterminacy, patient and watchful waiting, the reading of signs—these are Jewish ideas and characteristic of "the people of the book." Hartman's Hebraism, which I treated at some length in the previous chapter, appears as well, I suggest, in his opposition to turning "a book into a bible whose truth is revealed rather than read" (*STT,* p. 86). It appears too in his opposition to the Hellenic notion that the "spirit continually comes to rest, or arrests itself, in an object" (*STT,* p. 84); just as the Ark is always empty, so is the father absent and meaning dispersed rather than arrested in an object. As Bloom has written, meaning "is always wandering meaning, even as the Jews were a wandering people."[12] Like Buber, who so influenced the early Bloom, Hartman is more interested in relations than objects.

Hartman's reference in *Criticism in the Wilderness* to Beryl Smalley's *The Study of the Bible in the Middle Ages* allows me to move to my last point. In discussing this matter of artistic objects, Hartman makes this point, via Smalley, concerning allegorical exegesis: " 'It is as though we were invited to focus our eyes not on the physical surface of the object, but on infinity as seen through the lattice' " (p. 236). Thus continues Hartman, " 'we are invited to look not at the text, but through it'— which recalls William Blake's comment that the visionary poet looks through rather than with the eye" (*CW,* p. 236). We hear in such passages a Hebraic opposition to idolatry. If, as Hartman writes, Derrida's "*Glas* is of the House of Galilee," he is himself the Wandering Jew (*STT,* pp. 19, 144).

At any rate, Hartman's sense of reader-responsibility is deeply indebted to the responsibility exhibited by biblical exegetes, and he advocates a return to such practice. Thus in

Criticism in the Wilderness, lamenting the fact of "so little exegetical daring" (p. 4), he writes that "pleasure may return to
the critic if he imitates older, more sacred modes of commentary" (p. 176). More specifically: "We can only urge that readers, inspired by hermeneutic traditions, take back some of their
authority and become both creative and thoughtful. . . . The
rabbinical or patristic exegete was creative within a
scrupulosity as exacting as any invented by the extreme apos-
tles of the Catholic or Puritan conscience; he pretended not to
violate the letter of Scripture or else he took pleasure in the
strict counterpoint of letter and spirit, of apparent meaning and
recreative commentary" (p. 161). Hartman's description of the
interpreter calls to mind especially the Rabbis, for "as far afield
as their discussions carried them, no matter how many free
associations were spun out of a particular word or verse, the
Rabbis insisted on the letter; they never swerved from their
belief that the Oral tradition was embedded in the Written. They
maintained the general hermeneutical principle that 'no Biblical
text may be divorced from its simple meaning' but also that 'he
who translates a verse according to its literal form is a falsi-
fier.' "[13] The way in which for Orthodox Judaism, as well as for
the Kabbalah, commentary was part of the text and the text part
of the commentary is, of course, like Hartman's sense that
criticism is already *in* literature. Moreover, to cite but one more
analogue, Rabbi Akiba, to whom Hartman is drawn (his recent
volume of poems is entitled *Akiba's Children*), seems to have
anticipated Hartman's insistence on hearing the words within
words, for Akiba "held that every verse, indeed every word,
letter, particle, conjunction, repetition, every flourish and horn
of each letter (and assuredly every phoneme) held many meanings."[14]

What appears in the Rabbis is also everywhere present in
Hartman: a rejection of "either/or" in favor of "both/and." For
while insisting on the letter, the Midrash "was concerned with
off-centered phenomena such as word-play, anagrams, acros-

tics, bad jokes, things that seemed meaningless or insignificant."[15] In continuing, in displaced fashion, this mode of exegesis and hermeneutical speculation, Hartman exhibits responsibility to texts *and* to thought and understanding, shuttling between theory and practice, poems and ideas. His is work of critical importance, his last two books especially addressing readers and the current critical crisis, in perhaps a more responsible way than most of the rather shrill voices now clamoring for priority with their essentially reductive systems and keys to literary understanding. Hartman's plea for hermeneutical patience and reader-responsibility is eloquent and demanding. How do we answer his call?

4. J. Hillis Miller, Deconstruction, and the Recovery of Transcendence

Following publication of *Charles Dickens: The World of His Novels* (1958), *The Disappearance of God* (1963), and *Poets of Reality* (1965), J. Hillis Miller became known as one of the most knowledgeable and articulate spokesmen for religion in modern literature. These works, and others, not only testify powerfully to Miller's interest as a literary critic in religious questions, but they also reveal his own deep religious convictions. A member of what was originally the Society for Religion in Higher Education, Miller has frequently contributed to conferences dealing with the growing interest in literature and religion, and his work has been reprinted in collections on religion in modern literature.[1] As he put it in a subtle and judicious essay "Literature and Religion," written for the Modern Language Association volume on *Relations of Literary Study,* "the religious commitment of the critic, or lack of it, cannot be considered irrelevant to his work."[2]

Through the mid-1960s Miller wrote under the influence of the important Swiss critic Georges Poulet, a practitioner of the "criticism of consciousness." This critical method, which explores the existential situation of authors treated and which seeks to identify the critic's consciousness with the author's, is particularly interested in metaphysical and ontological questions and seemed quite congenial to, if not constitutive of, Miller's own religious inclinations. Beginning in the late 1960s, however, as attested by *The Form of Victorian Fiction* (1968) and the revision of an essay entitled "Georges Poulet's 'Criticism of Identification,'" Miller came under the influence of Jacques Derrida, the father of deconstruction. *Thomas Hardy: Distance and Desire* (1970), and more than two dozen subsequent essays on a variety of topics, including the recently published *Fiction and Repetition* (1982), reflect Miller's adoption of deconstructive critical procedures. Indeed, Miller has to a large extent been responsible for the growing prominence of deconstruction in America.

Does Miller's switch from Poulet to Derrida and to the "tradition of difference" entail a marked change in religious outlook? A careful study of Miller's criticism, both before and after this conversion, may allow us to penetrate more deeply than has been done before into the far-reaching implications of deconstruction, as well as to shed light on the critical odyssey of Miller himself.

As a way of beginning our consideration, I turn to one of the more recent attacks on deconstruction, for the attack appears in terms directly relevant to our concerns. Writing in the *Georgia Review*, Harold Fromm discusses the supposed absurdity and nihilism of this new movement: "When Derrida speaks in *Of Grammatology* of the 'End of the Book and the Beginning of Writing' he has described the present situation. But when the integrative whole symbolized by the book turns into the indeterminate and open-ended 'text' of 'writing,' we are in a world without value." Fromm goes on, "In methodology like this, the Logos has been discredited while in its place is offered a plenitude of psychological detritus in which all data, like sparrows and hairs, must not only be noticed but must be cherished as well. And since they are not being cherished by an absent God, they must be noticed and cherished by a seem-

ingly present Man. Formerly, value was derived from presentness in the consciousness of God. Can equally plausible value
be derived from mere presentness in the consciousness of
Man?"[3] Though Fromm's concern is admirable and his worry
perhaps understandable, his objection to deconstruction, at
least as embraced and practiced by Miller, is to those same
features of modernism this movement precisely appears to
confront. The charges Fromm brings against deconstruction
are, I shall attempt to show, based on a shallow understanding
of the principles involved. As a matter of fact, Fromm's attack
evidently stems from a desire to salvage transcendence; he
writes: "at present, in a period of 'absence,' with God beyond
the horizon, the very notion of transcendence becomes sus-
pect, if not unintelligible. . . . Without the assurance of 'presence,' it can no longer be believed that anything whatever
possesses unlimited value, nor do literary texts constitute an
exception."[4] Actually, Miller's critical journey is an attempt to
recover transcendence, lost by modernism.

    Miller's odyssey begins in his "Geneva" phase, which has
been studied by Sarah Lawall, Vernon Ruland, and Vincent B.
Leitch.[5] Certainly a most important aspect of Miller's work in
this phase is the recent history of Western consciousness,
which he traces in *The Disappearance of God* and *Poets of
Reality.* Focusing on De Quincey, Browning, Emily Brontë, Arnold, and Hopkins, the earlier book describes the absence of
God in the nineteenth century, culminating with the climax of
Hopkins's own spiritual journey, wherein he accepts the Catholic doctrine of the Real Presence and so, according to Miller,
rejects "three hundred and fifty years which seem to be taking
man inexorably toward the nihilism of Nietzsche's 'Gott ist
tot.' "[6] But if Miller sees Hopkins and other nineteenth-century
writers "stretched on the rack of a fading transcendentalism,"
his own belief at the time "in a progressing history of metaphysical insight,"[7] leads him toward a presence which fills the
absence experienced by the Victorians. He thus ends *The
Disappearance of God:*

Only in Browning, of the writers studied here, are there hints and anticipations of that recovery of immanence which was to be the inner drama of twentieth-century literature. Browning alone seems to have glimpsed the fact that the sad alternatives of nihilism and escape beyond the world could be evaded if man would only reject twenty-five hundred years of belief in the dualism of heaven and earth. If man could do this he might come to see that being and value lie in *this* world, in what is immediate, tangible, present to man, in earth, sun, sea, in the stars in their courses, and in what Yeats was to call "the foul-rag-and-bone shop of the heart." But Browning, like De Quincey, Arnold, Hopkins, and Emily Brontë, was stretched on the rack of a fading transcendentalism, and could reach a precious unity only by the most extravagant stratagems of the spirit.[8]

In *Poets of Reality* Miller goes beyond the point described here, tracing, in Conrad, Yeats, Eliot, Thomas, Stevens, and Williams, a "journey beyond nihilism toward a poetry of reality," a journey that the critic experiences from within and indeed parallels in his own being. The starting point, for the twentieth century, is the recognition that God is dead, murdered by humanistic egotism: "when God and the creation become objects of consciousness, man becomes a nihilist. Nihilism is the nothingness of consciousness when consciousness becomes the foundation of everything. Man the murderer of God and drinker of the sea of creation wanders through the infinite nothingness of his own ego. Nothing now has any worth except the arbitrary value he sets on things as he assimilates them into his consciousness. . . . In the emptiness left after the death of God, man becomes the sovereign valuer, the measure of all things."[9]

Escape from subjectivism, according to Miller, involves "following the path of nihilism to the end, [whereby] man confronts once again a spiritual power external to himself." Specifically, the mind must "efface itself before reality . . . abandoning the will to power over things."[10] Emerging here is a new ontology, the idea of God resembling that discussed in the 1960s by such theologians as Tillich, Altizer, and Dewart: "a God who is no longer transcendent or supreme, but immanent and omnipresent throughout reality."[11] As Miller stresses "a new dimension of intimacy"[12] wherein mind and world unite, obliterating the age-old dualism of subject and object, the idea of God reappears under a new name, described now as the living presence of reality. Thus, writes Miller, "God is not the stillness and distance of transcendence, off somewhere beyond or above his creation. He is everywhere, in all his plenitude. Eternity is here and now, in each man's heart, in each grain of sand and field mouse squeaking in the corn."[13] Just as the traditional image of God as a being out there somewhere was being excoriated by Bishop Robinson in *Honest to God* and the "death of God" theologians, Miller was attacking idealist thinking. His position shines through when he asserts that "Eliot can only become a Christian when he ceases to be an idealist."[14]

If Miller was committed to the idea of immanence even before he discussed its discovery in the six writers treated in *Poets of Reality,* it was shortly after publication of that book that he realized the inadequacy of this apparent solution. The point is especially clear when Miller's treatment of William Carlos Williams in that book is compared with that printed in 1970 in a special issue of *Daedalus.* In the book he had written, "In the work of Yeats, Thomas, and Stevens can be witnessed the difficult struggle to go beyond the old traditions. Williams goes farthest. He begins within the space of immanence and his work is a magnificent uncovering of its riches."[15] The 1970 essay takes up similar themes. In terms consonant with *Poets of Reality,* Miller writes that *"Spring and All* is based on an affirmation of the supreme value of presence and of the present, and on a repudiation of all that is derived, repetitive, and copied. . . . Authentic life exists only in the present moment of immediate experience.'' Miller argues, in fact, that Williams rejects whatever stands between man and ''the living moment'': symbolism, subjectivism, supernaturalism. This project Miller describes, somewhat problematically, as a version of the ''deconstruction of metaphysics.''[16] The result of Miller's return to Williams becomes distinctly Derridean as he shows how Williams's project fails. The hope had been for authentic creation, for the realization of a world pristine in its primal novelty. Realized, however, is a repetition of the way it has always been, a dead imitation. As in everything else, ''like the tradition lying behind it, [Williams's] theory of art is unable to free itself from the theories it rejects.''[17]

Williams's ''break'' with tradition, his deconstruction of metaphysics, his attempt to grasp immediate presence—these now point Miller in the direction charted by Derrida. Realizing that such deconstruction as Williams thought he was accomplishing can never be complete, that the belief one has broken out only reflects one's imprisonment, Miller writes, ''like Aristotle's *mimesis,* Williams's imagination is both part of and more than nature, both immediate and mediatorial—imitation, revelation, and creation at once. Like the long tradition he echoes, Williams remains caught in the inextricable web of connection among these concepts.''[18] Revealed in Williams's predicament is a point critical to Derridean thinking: the falsity of binary oppositions and all dualisms, inscribed in the Western tradition, because of the ''trace.'' Rather than the triumph of one term of an opposition over the other, as in our familiar dualisms, the ''trace,'' we now understand, keeps *differance* in play: the terms are inextricably linked, the one requiring the other, like host and parasite.[19]

Thus, contrary to the belief in progress and breakthrough expressed in *Poets of Reality,* Miller now writes that there is at once ''both progress and stasis.''[20] This is, in fact, the central issue in the *Daedalus* essay, designed to show that Williams did not, indeed could not wholly succeed in the project applauded in the book. In place of progress, breakthrough, and claimed undoing of traditions appears the humbling recognition that such undoing is also a preserving. Explaining the peculiar operation of *differance* with regard to his own work in the essay, Miller declares, "My interpretation, in its turn, both destroys the text it interprets and, I hope, revivifies it. Such a 'deconstruction' puts in question the received ideas of our tradition. At the same time my reading keeps the text alive by reliving it. It works back through its texture, repeats it once more in a different form, in a version of that transit through the texts of our heritage called for by Jacques Derrida." There is absolutely no "question of a breakthrough beyond metaphysics or of a 'reversal of Platonism.' This reversal has been performed over and over through the centuries, from the Stoics to Nietzsche and the radical philosophers of our own day, and yet Platonism still reigns. . . . There is no progress in human history, no unfolding or gradual perfection of the spirit. There are only endlessly varied ways to experience the human situation."[21]

Interestingly paralleling the essay on Williams and completed around the same time is Miller's revision of a 1963 essay on his old mentor, Poulet. In 1971 Miller reprints in shortened and slightly revised form that earlier laudatory piece, adding several pages of critical comment on Poulet to it and so dramatizing the Derridean position that one both undoes and preserves, at once. Miller now understands that Poulet is driven by the same desire as Williams: "the quality of *presence.*"[22] But again, despite his profound differences with Poulet, Miller knows better than to set up himself or Derrida as the opposite of Poulet. Statements like the following are crucial to an understanding of Miller's odyssey from "Geneva criticism" to deconstruction: "It would seem that the tradition represented by Derrida and that represented by Poulet must be set against one another as an irreconcilable either/or. A critic must choose either the tradition of presence or the tradition of 'difference,' for their assumptions about language, about literature, about history, and about the mind cannot be made compatible. The more deeply and carefully one reads Poulet's criticism, however, the more clearly it emerges that it challenges its own fundamental assumptions."[23] Difference within thus mitigates difference between. Moreover, though for Derrida not sameness but difference is primary, indeed originary, he shares with Poulet the important "reliving of the fundamental texts of our tradition,"[24] preserving as he undoes.

Just as no simple negative relation exists between Derrida and Poulet, so none exists between Miller's deconstructive and his earlier criticism. Miller himself affirms the point in a new preface written for the 1975 reprinting of *The Disappearance of God.* He writes, "I am no longer quite the same person I was when I wrote it, and I would not write it in quite the same way today. [Still] I find myself . . . more or less in agreement with the interpretations I proposed of my five authors."[25] The conclusion, in any case, is the same as that reached in the Williams essay and the 1971 piece on Poulet: "it appears that the relation between my present work and that of over a decade ago is more than simply negative. It may be in the nature of literature that investigations of it initiated according to a given hypothesis will lead, if carried far enough, to insights which call that hypothesis into question."[26]

Now, because of the "trace," the presence and immanence Miller had earlier yearned for, and indeed posited, are apparently inseparable from the absence and transcendence he thought he was going beyond. Transcendence reappears, however, not merely as the inescapable "opposite" of immanence; it may be manifest also in deconstruction's basic principle of undoing/preserving. Precisely in this fashion deconstruction suggests, despite the charges of Harold Fromm and others, one route to the recovery of transcendence that Western man has long craved. For if undoing produces the realization that what we thought of as ground, as reality, is no ground, then have we not with that awareness transcended the "real," if only momentarily? With difference, of course, a gap forever remains, completion and identity being impossible this side of death.

Interestingly, as early as his first book, in 1958, Miller glimpsed the sense of transcendence I am suggesting. There he wrote, referring to *Great Expectations,* that Pip "must accept the fact that he can in no way transcend the gap between 'the small bundle of shivers growing afraid of it all and beginning to cry' and the wind, sun, sky, and marshland, the alien universe—in no way, that is, but by willingly accepting this situation."[27] In the same book, Miller even shows awareness of the value in tracing nihilism through to the end, of the validity of Chesterton's remark that you know nothing until you know nothing, writing that "Dickens' last heroes and heroines come back to life after a purifying descent into the dark waters of death, but they come back to assume just that situation which was given one in society. The difference is that their contact with the negative transcendence has liberated them to a new attitude toward their situation."[28] Miller puts essentially the same point in figurative terms, smacking of the biblical, in discussing *Our Mutual Friend:* "When one has recognized that gold is dust, one can go on to make gold of dust. Out of dust can come gold, out of death, life. Gold forced upon us, or accepted as an absolute value in itself, is dust, but so long as we are free to value the world we can make gold."[29]

The significance of these crucial points concerning transcendence Miller apparently did not at that time fully grasp; to take one of his favorite metaphors, they were threads in the critical fabric he wove, but not ones he chose to follow through to their end. By the late 1960s Miller was more aware that the way of seeing is all, and as a Derridean emphasized in *The Form of Victorian Fiction* what he had previously only glimpsed:

> Each man must return from an encounter with ["the ele-
> mental realities of death, physical nature, and human
> feeling"] to reengage himself in society. This new involve-
> ment will be made from the perspective of a prior disen-
> gagement which sees society as it is. This means
> reentering society by improvising one's role in it as a
> game. Society cannot be anything but a system of con-
> ventional rules, exchanges, and substitutions which are
> like metaphors. As long as a man takes the metaphor
> as reality he is deluded. When he sees through the met-
> aphor and takes responsibility for living according to it,
> he is still caught in a play, but now he sees the game as
> a game.[30]

Undoing/preserving, this vision is transcendent. It is thus liber-
ating, allowing one to build and create but always with the
awareness that that created is a human fabrication.

Clarification of, as well as support for, my point that deconstruction hopes to recover transcendence appears if we
broaden our treatment to take in others influenced by Derrida.
In the work of one of these, John Dominic Crossan, a biblical
scholar and literary critic, the metaphor of play that Miller uses
in the quotation above functions to herald transcendence. Thus
Crossan writes in *The Dark Interval: Towards a Theology of
Story,* which I cited earlier in a different context, that "the
excitement of transcendental experience is found only at the
edge of language and the limit of story and . . . the only way
to find that excitement is to test those edges and those limits."[31] Parables do this supremely well, revealing the possibility
of transcendence. They

> give God room. The parables of Jesus are *not* historical
> allegories telling us how God acts with mankind; neither
> are they moral example-stories telling us how to act be-
> fore God and towards one another. They are stories

which shatter the deep structure of our accepted world
and thereby render clear and evident to us the relativity
of story itself. They remove our defences and make us
vulnerable to God. It is only in such experiences that God
can touch us, and only in such moments does the king-
dom of God arrive. My own term for this relationship is
transcendence.[32]

The point here is the subversion of final words about "reality,"
thus the recognition of the fictionality of all things, and the
freedom, the ability to let go, that follows therefrom.

Like Derrida and Miller, Crossan agrees with Roland Barthes
that "literature is unreality itself; . . . far from being an analogi-
cal copy of reality, *literature is on the contrary the very consciousness of the unreality of language.*"[33] He pursues this
insight, developing the implications of *The Dark Interval,* in a
book on comic eschatology in Jesus and Borges. Focusing
again on game and story, Crossan aims to dismantle eschatology and recover transcendence through an intense focus on biblioclasm. That is, he shows how Jesus extends
Mosaic iconoclasm into language itself; Jesus' language thus
"is an attack on form within all the major traditions of Israel's
inheritance. Such content is intrinsically eschatological, forcing
world and language to its knees before the aniconic God of
Israel."[34] More specifically, insisting that it is "only by a full and
glad acceptance of our utter finitude [that we can] experience
authentic transcendence," Crossan seems to echo Miller. Jesus, he says, uses "paradoxical aphorism or antiproverb to
point us beyond proverb and beyond wisdom by reminding us
that making it all cohere is simply one of our more intriguing
human endeavors and that God is often invoked to buttress the
invented coherence. There is nothing wrong," adds Crossan,
"with making a whole of one's existence as long as one does
it in conscious knowledge that world is our supreme play and
that we encounter the Holy in its eschatology."[35] As with Miller,

then, transcendence reappears, this time as a leap into the darkness, as a self-conscious way of seeing.

The work of Herbert N. Schneidau makes even clearer the possible congruence of deconstruction and biblical thought. In his marvelously rich and suggestive *Sacred Discontent,* Schneidau brings into subtle and illuminating synthesis results from biblical archaeology, contemporary anthropology, history, and literary criticism and argues Derrida's indebtedness to the Yahwist vision. According to Schneidau, as I noted earlier, the Bible, literature, and Derridean thought share a characteristic ambivalence, what I have been calling the undoing/preserving central to deconstruction. Thus, just as the Hebrews both criticize and nourish culture in their "sacred discontent," so literature, in Pound's phrase, goes on trying to "make it new" even as it knows the impossibility, bequeathing to the West a strongly Hebraic sense despite Hellenistic influence.[36] The key, as with Miller, Crossan, and Schneidau, seems to lie in recognizing the fictionality of all things, by which transcendence is achieved. Miller aligns himself directly with the positions articulated by Schneidau and Crossan, writing in "Tradition and Difference" that "there would appear to be no escape from the prison of language except by way of a radical theory of fictions and of the interpretation of fictions."[37]

With the condition carefully traced by Miller whereby the human consciousness "becomes the foundation of everything," man is in obvious need of such decentering as Schneidau describes the Bible as providing. As we have seen, deconstruction, like the Bible, becomes a valuable agent of the demythologization of some of our most cherished stabilities. We may gradually realize that our grand schemes of order are fictional constructs made by ourselves and the vanity of human wishes. Even the self that we seek to protect and that itself seeks to be the measure of all things turns out to be a fictional construct. For deconstruction, in contrast to the autonomous consciousness of modernism, posits no single self but several selves. If the self is a linguistic construction, coming into being in and through language rather than preceding and being simply expressed by language, we may have to rethink personality in terms of *personae.*

Consonant with the biblical tradition, at least as it is described by Crossan, Schneidau, and others, deconstruction offers a way to transcend the nihilism that Miller finds in twentieth-century life and literature and that Fromm for one condemns. Indeed, deconstruction appears to offer an alternative to nihilism that escapes the difficulties posed by the "solution" reached in *Poets of Reality.* For the immanence praised there seems caught unaware in the metaphysical system of binary oppositions and so trapped in desire of presence. Transcendence, understood in the ways I have discussed, is rooted in the necessary awareness both of the seductive and pervasive lure of presence and of its impossibility. J. Hillis Miller may have found attractive such transcendence as deconstruction points to. He shows, in my view at least, continuing Christian concern.

PART TWO

Reading Deconstruction Becomes Deconstructive Reading

5. The Story of Error

Vincent B. Leitch's essay "The Lateral Dance: The Deconstructive Criticism of J. Hillis Miller" is an admirably full, sympathetic, and therefore welcome treatment of this important critic and of deconstruction generally.[1] But despite Leitch's obviously wide reading in deconstruction and his close familiarity with Miller's texts, he seems to have mistaken some crucial points. Miller's response to Leitch in the same journal ("Theory and Practice," pp. 609-14), though often helpful in quarreling with emphases, may not confront forcefully enough certain major problems. In order that these misconceptions not go virtually unchallenged, I offer the following response. More is at stake, however, than Leitch's apparent errors concerning Miller and deconstruction. A close reading of the essays, especially as they are related to each other, involves us in such large issues as the nature of choice, the relation of critic and text, the possibility of reading, and the nature of error.

I begin with Leitch's account of Miller as a "nihilistic magician" (p. 603). Though Miller is obviously, and rightly, troubled by this frequent charge, he neglects to make certain points in response, and even his most forthright objection is not sharply enough focused. I have argued in the previous chapter that Miller's far-from-simple critical odyssey from "criticism of consciousness" to deconstruction, from the prevailing influence of Poulet to that of Derrida, traces an abiding concern, present from the beginning, to find an adequate alternative to the nihilism of what is usually called modernity. Deconstruction may be precisely that desired alternative, or at least the path toward it. In a recent essay, "The Critic as Host," Miller makes a direct assault on nihilism, showing how it is not the opposite but rather the dark side of metaphysics, not outside but within metaphysics.[2] As he says in "Theory and Practice," "one of the aims of deconstruction is precisely to free us from the false specter of nihilism" (p. 613). Leitch, however, appears not to grasp how nihilism and metaphysics inhabit each other, like "host" and "parasite," terms that—as Miller demonstrates—have no meaning in the other's absence. Rather than with nihilism, deconstruction might better be associated with the "sacred discontent" of the biblical (or at least Yahwist) vision, as I suggested earlier.

Leitch's error concerning deconstruction and nihilism may be taken as a synecdoche of other apparent confusions in the essay. To see Miller and deconstruction as nihilistic is not only to misconstrue them but also to write from and with the blindness of the metaphysical tradition that Miller and his colleagues put in question. This particular blindness appears throughout Leitch's essay. Like that of another recent essay on Miller,[3] Leitch's error often takes the form of projecting onto Miller the very oppositional thinking that he himself exhibits but that Miller and such fellow deconstructionists as Derrida and de Man are engaged in deconstructing. In his response, Miller alludes to the problem in objecting to Leitch's separating theory from the particular readings he has produced. Unfortunately, Miller does not develop the point. Development might, however, take some such form as the following: Deconstructive criticism involves at once and inextricably both theory and practice (this involvement is a feature of Miller's own deconstructive labors).[4] Rather than related as hierarchical oppositions, as Leitch suggests, theory and practice are regarded in deconstruction as interimplicating each other. To separate them in Leitch's fashion is to exempt theory from the necessity of interpretation, placing it outside the play of language as a controlling center, privileging it as a Transcendental Signified. Discussing another but structurally similar issue, Miller makes the point succinctly: "The relation is a triangle, not a polar opposition. There is always a third to whom the two are related, something before them or between them . . . across which they meet."[5] The "trace" may be this "third," keeping language forever in play, insuring the perpetual oscillation of meanings, and deconstructing our usual way of thinking in simple oppositions, such as theory and practice. Leitch is both close to and far from recognizing the fundamental point when he writes: "Essentially, Derrida shows in *Of Grammatology* how certain binary oppositions, especially 'nature/culture,' are illusory" (p. 599). The Derridean point is, of course, that *all* binary oppositions are illusory. Because of the "trace" and *differance,* the so-called oppositions are linked, each member having no meaning without the other, indeed requiring the other. Is either /or therefore really both/and?

At issue is the nature of choice. Glimpsed in Leitch's privileging of theory, as well as in the question of nihilism, is the commitment to either/or thinking that is stated explicitly elsewhere in the essay. Leitch opens with an epigraph, one sentence from a 1971 essay by Miller, "Georges Poulet's 'Criticism of Identification.' " Though I have already cited the passage, I must here quote that sentence and the two surrounding it:

It would seem that the tradition represented by Derrida and that represented by Poulet must be set against one another as an irreconcilable either/or. A critic must choose either the tradition of presence or the tradition of "difference," for their assumptions about language, about literature, about history, and about the mind cannot be made compatible. The more deeply and carefully one reads Poulet's criticism, however, the more clearly it

emerges that it challenges its own fundamental assumptions and that as his work gradually develops it encoun-
ters in its own way the same problematical issues which
are central for a critic like Derrida.[6]

Referring to the second sentence quoted here, Leitch comments: "These words of J. Hillis Miller make us slightly uncom-
fortable because they demand that we choose one tradition or
another. Without question, the decision involves the 'whole
shebang.' This succinctly formulated 'either/or' choice not only
asks us to take a stand but foregrounds for us a fundamental
rift in contemporary critical theory" (p. 593). But does Miller's
text establish here an either/or situation and demand a simple
choice? I think not. The one sentence Leitch quotes may be a
statement affirming the necessity of choice, but then again it
may be only an elaboration from the point of view of the previous sentence. In the first case, the sentence Leitch quotes
would be seen as indicating Miller's own position but in the
second as merely exemplifying a position Miller does not accept. Especially in light of the "however" in the third sentence
I have quoted, the second appears a possible reading.
Other considerations support the argument that Miller does not
here simply place terms, influences, and traditions in either/or
opposition but rather sees their complications and recognizes
their involvement in one another. What, after all, is this particular essay by Miller? A reprinting of an earlier, laudatory essay
on Poulet with the addition of several pages of critical comment, it is a dramatization of the undoing/preserving oscillation
that characterizes Miller's recent thinking and that of deconstruction generally.[7] As to the matter of the rival traditions,
perhaps, as Paul de Man puts it, they "compel us to choose
while destroying the foundations of any choice."[8] We may have
to choose, in other words, but the choice is far from simple—
for reasons we may better understand as we continue our
reading of Leitch's essay.[9]

Some disturbing implications of Leitch's understanding of deconstruction emerge clearly by the end of his essay. Again transferring his own "metaphysical" or logocentric perspective to the texts being discussed, Leitch writes: "The deconstructer does not simply enter a work with an attentive eye for the loose thread or the alogical element that will decenter the text; he or she intends *beforehand* to reverse the traditional hierarchies that constitute the ground of the text" (p. 605). Evidently Leitch's "deconstructer" is little interested in the text at hand, which by his account is merely being used for an extrinsic—and de-structive—purpose. The will of the "deconstructer" is thus imposed, forced upon the text, for he or she treats it as slave to the interpreter-master, establishing the will as a controlling center, exempt like theory from the necessity of interpretation. In this fashion the "deconstructer" halts the play of language. Such is far from the goal of the deconstructive criticism produced by Miller, Derrida, and de Man, at least as I understand it. On this important point Miller writes in "Theory and Practice": "the readings of deconstructive criticism are not the willful imposition by a subjectivity of theory on the texts but are coerced by the texts themselves" (p. 611).[10]

At least one other problem appears in my last quotation from Leitch, and that is his desire "to reverse the traditional hierarchies." That desire reemerges later as he writes: "the project of deconstruction is ultimately to . . . put . . . the 'tradition of difference' in place of the now dominant 'tradition of presence'" (pp. 605-6). Though he wants to overturn more than two thousand years of logocentric thinking, Leitch uses the very language that confirms and perpetuates the tradition he hopes to displace. This is "the impasse of deconstruction," which Leitch himself well describes: "Unable to go beyond language, the deconstructer is compelled to use the concepts and figures of the metaphysical tradition" (p. 606). True, but of course the critic has the responsibility to be as scrupulous and rigorous as possible and should not easily let pass as deconstruction what deconstruction precisely puts in question. To return now to the previous quotations from Leitch: Like William E. Cain, who, in his essay on Miller, looks toward "a thorough-going deconstruction,"[11] radically different from that of the Yale group, Leitch would enforce closure. Aiming to undermine and undo, Leitch seems not to realize that any undoing is also and at once a preserving. To attempt merely to replace one term in a hierarchy with another is to remain within hierarchical and oppositional (that is, metaphysical, logocentric) thinking. As Derrida makes clear in various texts, the "project" is not simply to invert the hierarchy, which would only confirm the categories, but to transform the notion of hierarchy itself. According to Derrida, overthrowing the hierarchy is only a "first" (though of course necessary) step: "to remain in this phase is still to operate on the terrain of and from within the deconstructed system."[12] Miller repeatedly makes the same point. Note, for instance, his "Stevens' Rock and Criticism as Cure, II," where he differentiates between "canny" (i.e., logical, Apollonian) and "uncanny" (i.e., "tragic," Dionysian) critics, momentarily reversing the hierarchy by which we customarily elevate the "canny."[13] Then Miller proceeds to the step that Derrida insists on but that Leitch and Cain neglect to take. Rather than stop the movement once the reversal is effected, Miller continues the play: just as he did in the 1971 essay on Poulet and Derrida, Miller shows, by carefully attending to both what a text declares and what it describes, how one is the accomplice of the other; pressed sufficiently, the "uncanny" turns into the "canny," the "canny" into the "uncanny."[14] At the very least this situation complicates the nature of choice.

What happens in "Stevens' Rock and Criticism as Cure, II" and elsewhere in deconstructive criticism is thus much more than, and different from, simple inversion. What distinguishes deconstruction from what may be called de-struction is precisely that the movement or play does not stop with an initial reversal. As with the "uncanny," the newly elevated term is reinscribed in the field of language and shown to oscillate ceaselessly with its apparent opposite. Thus to reverse the hierarchy only so as to displace the reversal; to unravel in order to reconstitute what is always already inscribed. Therefore, as Miller wrote in 1970, there is no "question of a breakthrough beyond metaphysics or of a 'reversal of Platonism.' This reversal has been performed over and over through the centuries, from the Stoics to Nietzsche and the radical philosophers of our own day, and yet Platonism still reigns."[15]

The point I wish to stress is not simply that Leitch has mistaken certain important directions in deconstruction. We approach the more interesting, and revealing, questions when we recognize the *nature* of Leitch's errors and understand that his text also "challenges its own fundamental assumptions." In spite of his obvious desire to be "uncanny" and to align himself with the "tradition of 'difference,'" he displays the very thinking he opposes, his text describing an argument that links him with the tradition of identity and presence. Indeed, the two traditions are at war in his essay. This means, for one thing, that Leitch's essay both affirms and denies its declared argument concerning the possibility of a clear and simple choice between, for instance, rival traditions. "The Lateral Dance" is, then, unreadable: its described argument contends with the declared argument, and there is no way to assign priority or determine preference. As to the errors, they are more than errors of "fact" to be empirically checked and perhaps corrected; they are of such a kind as to tell a story. In this case, a story of error becomes the story of error. Leitch's essay tells the story of error, of the inevitability of error due to the dialogical (both/and) nature of literary texts and to our choosing between two equally cogent but mutually exclusive meanings, either of which can be deconstructed and put in question in terms of the other.

Suppose, though, that Leitch could be prevailed upon to rewrite his essay, taking account of my criticism above, elimi-

nating the "factual" errors noted, and being less "metaphysical" in his declarations. Would that less mystified version also
be the story of error? Leitch himself suggests that it would, in
discussing "the impasse of deconstruction." I have made the
same claim. The existence of Miller's own essays, on which
Leitch's is based, and of Miller's response provides a good
opportunity to verify that claim. As we shall see, Miller's own
texts, including "Theory and Practice," do not escape the wandering of "truth." In no sense can they stand as primary truth
over against his commentator's secondary errors. Even though
Miller fully grasps deconstructive principles that Leitch apparently misunderstands, he nonetheless produces similarly bifurcated texts. Though the critic has the responsibility to be as
wary and as rigorous as he possibly can, the issue is not finally
one of competence, enlightenment, or will. It is perhaps only
the degree of obviousness with which the error is committed.
And indeed, no less than Leitch's essay, Miller's texts are the
story of error.[16]

To illustrate the point I choose first a passage in Miller's
essay "Ariachne's Broken Woof," from which Leitch quotes.
There Miller writes: "Deconstruction . . . attempts to reverse the
implicit hierarchy within the terms in which the dialogical has
been defined. It attempts to define the monological, the logocentric, as a derived effect of the dialogical rather than as the
noble affirmation of which the dialogical is a disturbance, a
secondary shadow in the originating light. Deconstruction attempts a crisscross substitution of early and late."[17] Though
the last sentence here suggests the endless oscillating movement that I described above, the first seems to sanction
Leitch's conclusion that deconstruction is a de-structive
"project." In that first sentence (the only one Leitch quotes),
Miller states a willingness simply to reverse hierarchies, rather
than proceed from that necessary step to reinscribe the reversal. Like Leitch's, Miller's text thus describes the kind of thinking that his essay elsewhere—and mainly—confronts and puts
in question.

The same is true of Miller's response to Leitch. Like all other texts, "Theory and Practice" is heterogeneous, containing assumptions that challenge its own argument, not mere contradictions but internal, fundamental differences that put the entire argument in question. Consider the following statement, which I quoted earlier: "the readings of deconstructive criticism are not the willful imposition by a subjectivity of theory on the texts but are coerced by the texts themselves" (p. 611). Obviously, Miller wants to challenge Leitch's notion that in deconstruction readings are subject to the interpreter's will. But his "correction" is the flip-side of Leitch's error. That is, in denying that texts are slaves to the interpreter-master and his imported theory by simply inverting Leitch's hierarchy, retaining the either /or choice, and making the interpreter slave to the text-master, Miller exhibits again the kind of thinking that we found in Leitch's essay. For Miller in this passage the choice is simply either/or: are readings "coerced" by the texts themselves or by the interpreter and his theory? Thus Leitch's essay and Miller's response posit two either/or choices that differ only in respect to the preference stated. Hierarchized thinking remains intact.

In the oscillating movement between "opposed" terms that defines deconstruction, however, the relationship between critic and text is understood differently, indeed differentially. Seeking neither to destroy nor to refute and under no illusion about setting up a new "answer," deconstruction, as I understand it, is simply a quest. A quest that is also a question, deconstruction requires a movement and an asking, a willful movement and a willful imposition of the question by a will-ing critic. To ask a question of a text is an attempt to coerce a response; it is an attempt to make the "respondent" willing to answer. But the response from the text, which is also will-ing, is incomplete at best, and that serves merely to create additional questions. Imposition thus occurs, and it comes from both critic and text. What emerges is a battle of wills between text and critic—a dialogue of questions that is a mutual coercion. Mutually dependent on language, critic and text question each other, read each other. They are thus caught in an inevitable and ceaseless oscillation in which neither text nor critic dominates, acts as master to the slave-other.

This last point is necessarily applicable to Leitch's essay and to Miller's response: neither is master or slave to the other. Together the essays dramatize the oscillating struggle for mastery that exists between critic and text as Leitch reads Miller, who in turn reads him. And each essay is, in its own way, the story of error, a wandering, an allegory. By now we understand that the real quest(ion) is not of an error to be corrected. Error —wandering (and wondering)—is inevitable, no matter how careful and rigorous one is. Deconstruction looks at *(theoria)* error, reading the story told by the wandering of "truth," and is itself just as error-ridden as any other writing. De Man makes the last point succinctly; dealing with rhetorical defigurations, he writes that deconstructive readings are "powerless" to prevent "in their own discourse, and to uncross, so to speak, the aberrant exchanges that have taken place." They can only repeat what "caused the error in the first place. They leave a margin of error, a residue of logical tension that prevents the closure of the deconstructive discourse and accounts for its narrative and allegorical mode."[18] The essays by Leitch and Miller tell this story.

PART THREE

Deconstructive Reading

6. Reading and/as Swerving:

The Quest(ion) of Interpretive Authority in Dryden's *Religio Laici*

As I have argued in a recent book, in *Religio Laici* Dryden cleverly and skillfully uses the "layman's faith" tradition, trying to deflect it from its inherent individualism to a ringing celebration of an ultimate authority outside the self.[1] Like many other texts of the Augustan period, Dryden's layman's faith is designed to convince man of his own insufficiency and to "guide" him "upward" so that he recognize his absolute dependency on God. Despite man's vain, proud attempt to soar "by his own strength to Heaven" and "not be Oblig'd to God for more" (ll. 62-63), Dryden argues, we can finally expect little relief "from *humane Wit"*: "sadly are we sure / *Still* to be *Sick,* till *Heav'n* reveal the *Cure"* (ll. 118-20).[2] That cure is Scripture, the *"Will reveal'd"* (l. 123), and *Religio Laici* enacts a movement taking the reader, via its several specific arguments, to that text as the authoritative Word of God. Attempting to be authoritative itself in reading that authority, *Religio Laici* focuses on problems in reading and interpretation.

Reading Henry Dickinson's recent translation of Father

Richard Simon's *Critical History of the Old Testament,* Dryden writes, "bred" his own efforts in *Religio Laici* (I. 226), and we shall see that, just as Dryden reads "against the grain" of this Catholic book, finding it, in spite of itself, a description of the way *"Jewish, Popish,* Interests have prevail'd, / And where *Infallibility* has *fail'd"* (II. 250-51), our own close attention to Dryden's text will reveal a description that fundamentally challenges his declarations. The relationship between declaration and description, text and reader, one reading and another, is our concern here. Though what I write here differs considerably from what I have written elsewhere on the poem, I do not think the relation between that earlier writing and the present simply negative (the situation is obviously analogous to Miller's rewriting of his essay on Poulet). Such relations are, at the very least, complicated.

Both the poem that is *Religio Laici or A Laymans Faith* and its prose Preface stress that Scripture is "the Canon of our Faith" and that as such "in all things needfull to Salvation, it is clear, sufficient, and ordain'd by God Almighty for that purpose" (p. 102). By so asserting, Dryden says, he has "unavoidably created to my self two sorts of Enemies: The Papists indeed, more directly, because they have kept the Scripture from us, what they cou'd; and have reserv'd to themselves a right of Interpreting what they have deliver'd under the pretense of Infalibility: and the Fanaticks more collaterally, because they have assum'd what amounts to an Infalibility, in the private Spirit: and have detorted those Texts of Scripture, which are not necessary to Salvation, to the damnable uses of Sedition, disturbance and destruction of the Civil Government" (ibid.). Several points are to be noted here, including the political nature of Dryden's concern, his implicit claim that essential parts of Scripture are so clear as to offer no opportunity for misreading and abuse, and, most important, the close similarities Dryden finds between the Papists and the Fanatics. In his view the issue is one of authority: is the biblical text itself the final authority, or does that reside in either the church or the private spirit, the Papists having declared an infallibility in the former, the Fanatics a like infallibility in the latter?

According to Dryden, the Bible, the ultimate authority, has long been enslaved to the will of one or another powerful force. In keeping Scripture from the laity, the Catholics enslaved both text and lay readers to the interpretive authority of the clergy. Dryden writes:

> In times o'ergrown with Rust and Ignorance,
> A gainfull Trade their Clergy did advance:
> When want of Learning kept the *Laymen* low,
> And none but *Priests* were *Authoriz'd* to *know:*
> When what small Knowledge was, in them did dwell;
> And he a *God* who cou'd but *Reade* or *Spell;*
> Then *Mother Church* did mightily prevail:
> She parcel'd out the Bible by *retail:*
> But still *expounded* what She *sold* or *gave;*
> To keep it in *her Power* to *Damn* and *Save:*
> *Scripture* was *scarce,* and as the Market went,
> Poor *Laymen* took *Salvation* on *Content;*
> As needy men take Money, good or bad:
> *God's* Word they had not, but the *Priests* they had.
> Yet, whate'er *false Conveyances* they made,
> The *Lawyer* still was *certain* to be paid.
> In those dark times they learn'd their knack so well,
> That by long use they grew *Infallible:*
> At last, a knowing Age began t' enquire
> If *they* the *Book,* or *That* did *Them* inspire:
> And, making narrower search they found, thô late,
> That what they thought the *Priest*'s, was *Their* Estate:
> Taught by the *Will produc'd,* (the written Word)
> How long they had been *cheated* on *Record.*

Then, every man who saw the Title fair,
Claim'd a Child's part, and put in for a Share:
Consulted Soberly his private good;
And sav'd himself as cheap as e'er he cou'd.
                                        (ll. 370-97)

When the Protestants broke free of Catholic domination and
Scripture was put "in every vulgar hand," "each presum'd he
best cou'd understand" it, the result being that "The *Common
Rule* was made the *common Prey*" (ll. 400-2). Now "The
Spirit gave the *Doctoral Degree:* / And every member of a
Company / Was of *his Trade,* and of the *Bible free*" (ll.
406-8.) Unwilling to content themselves with "Plain *Truths,*"
the newly freed slaves thus repeated their former masters'
tactics and actions, similarly occluding the Word of God
through an "itching to expound" (ll. 409-10). Dryden con-
cludes, therefore:

So all we make of Heavens discover'd Will
Is, not to have it, or to use it ill.
The Danger's much the same; on several Shelves
If *others* wreck *us,* or *we* wreck our *selves.*
                                        (ll. 423-26)

The historical sketch Dryden gives shows, then, that the text,
in his view the true authority, has long been enslaved to the
reader, whether Catholic churchman or Protestant layman. The
text itself, of course, has a will, and Dryden specifically refers
to Scripture as a will. Naturally conflict results when God's will
and the human will meet. Dryden's aim is to subject the latter
to the authority of the former.

I hope it is clear that the terms of power and struggle are the
text's and not simply my own. They also appear, incidentally,
in the commendatory poems affixed to early editions of *Religio
Laici.* In one of these, John Lord Vaughan writes that, thanks
to Dryden's efforts, "Freely we now may buy the Pearl of price"

(l.17), and in another, Thomas Creech asserts that "Triumphant Faith now takes a nobler course, / 'Tis gentle, but resists intruding force" (ll. 5-6); Dryden, he claims, has freed the laity "from a double Care" (l. 19).[3] And in the last of these verses, the Earl of Roscommon writes:

> While mighty *Lewis* finds the *Pope* too Great,
> And dreads the Yoke of his imposing Seat,
> Our Sects a more Tyrannick Power assume,
> And would for Scorpions change the Rods of *Rome.*
> That Church detain'd the Legacy Divine;
> Fanaticks cast the Pearls of Heaven to Swine:
> What then have honest thinking men to doe,
> But chuse a mean between th' Usurping two?
>
> (ll. 11-18)

Religio Laici thus addresses the far-reaching implications of the freedom of interpretation ushered in by Protestantism. Indeed, Dryden espouses an essentially lay position on reading Scripture, certainly rejecting the interpretive authority of the church and the priesthood. But he also denies the authority of the individual reader, minimizing the authority of the church not in order to set up "a *Pope* in every private mans breast"[4] but only to elevate the Ultimate Authority, which is God alone. Thus he insists on the authority of the text itself. Confronting both the Catholic position that Scripture is unclear even on essential points and so in need of priestly interpretation as well as the Miltonic argument, in *De Christiana Doctrina,* that "Scripture is merely an external guide that must give way to the Spirit within us,"[5] Dryden writes:

> The *Book*'s a *Common Largess* to *Mankind;*
> Not more for *them* [the Catholics] than *every* Man
>   design'd:
> The *welcome News* is in the *Letter* found;
> The *Carrier*'s not commission'd to *expound.*

It *speaks* it *Self,* and what it does contain,
In all things *needfull* to be *known,* is *plain.*
(ll. 364-69)

He thus argues that the layman have access to Scripture *and*
that he accept responsibility for allowing the text to "speak
itself." Directed toward his particular ends, Dryden's argument
is the Protestant one of Archbishop Tillotson that "our Principle
is, That the Scripture doth sufficiently interpret it self, that is, is
plain to all capacities, in things necessary to be believed and
practised" and of the Dissenter Henry Care that "the Infallible
Rule of the Interpretation of Scripture is the Scripture it self."[6]
The usual name for the Protestant principle alluded to by Tillotson and Care and operative in *Religio Laici* is *Scriptura sola.*

Dryden bases his particular argument for the ultimate authority of Scripture on its supposed clarity and self-sufficiency:
because the text *"speaks* it *Self,* and what it does contain, /
In all things *needfull* to be *known,* is *plain,"* the reader cannot
claim interpretive authority—unless in blatant and perverse
willfulness; and as we saw earlier, Dryden suggests in the
Preface that the essential parts of Scripture are so plain as to
make misreading next to impossible, no matter how strong the
desire. As a reader himself, now responding in writing to his
reading of Dickinson's translation of Father Simon's seminal
scholarly work on the Old Testament, Dryden claims that "from
Sacred Truth I do not swerve" (l. 455). As a matter of fact, his
own effort in *Religio Laici* is intended as a parallel to the
claimed plainness, directness, and literalness of Scripture:
"this unpolish'd, rugged Verse, I chose; / As fittest for Discourse, and nearest Prose" (ll. 453-54).

Dryden's aim is, of course, to keep readers from swerving
from *"Sacred Truth,"* as he claims he has been able to do. But
in the Preface he indicates that it is not merely misreading and
willfulness that blot out the Word of God; there is something
dangerous and diverting about language itself which allows
swerving to occur: and that is figuration. To be direct and

unswerving, Dryden writes, one must avoid figurative language: "The Expressions of a Poem, design'd purely for Instruction, ought to be Plain and Natural, and yet Majestick: for here the Poet is presum'd to be a kind of Law-giver, and those three qualities which I have nam'd are proper to the Legislative style. The Florid, Elevated and Figurative way is for the Passions; for Love and Hatred, Fear and Anger, are begotten in the Soul by shewing their Objects out of their true proportion; either greater than the Life, or less; but Instruction is to be given by shewing them what they naturally are" (p. 109). Though in *Religio Laici* Dryden relies heavily on figuration (see the *exordium,* for example) and definite emotional appeals, carefully modulating the strength and intensity of his declamations (e.g., ll. 64-65, 93-98), in this passage he opposes to each other the legislative and the figurative, implying that they are essentially different and that they can be kept distinct. Dryden claims to be a truth-teller and law-giver himself, repeating the Scriptural message. In the mastery his friend Roscommon spoke of in a commendatory poem ("Begone you Slaves, you idle Vermin go, / Fly from the Scourges, and your Master know," ll. 1-2), the legislative poet moves into the center occupied by God and His Scripture.

Yet—apparently in spite of himself and certainly in more than one way—Dryden does swerve. The question is whether he swerves "from *Sacred Truth,*" but then perhaps God's text swerves also. In approaching an answer, we might note, first, that at a crucial point in his argument, Dryden swerves, acknowledging that, despite his claims, the Protestant principle of *Scriptura sola* is finally unsatisfactory. Indeed, Dryden's action reveals that this vaunted principle is vulnerable in precisely the way his opponents claimed—on the fundamental issue of Christ's nature. (Incidentally, I make many of these points in my book on Dryden, though I did not at the time grasp their deconstructive force.[7]) The turn occurs in Dryden's response to the following issue:

We hold, and say we prove from Scripture plain,
That *Christ* is *GOD;* the bold *Socinian*
From the *same* Scripture urges he's but *MAN.*
Now what Appeal can end th' important Suit?
Both parts *talk* loudly, but the *Rule* is *mute.*
(ll. 311-15)

Dryden then proceeds:

Shall I speak plain, and in a Nation free
Assume an honest *Layman's Liberty?*
I think (according to my little Skill,)
(To my own Mother-Church submitting still)
That many have been sav'd, and many may,
Who never heard this Question brought in play.
Th' *unletter'd* Christian, who believes in *gross,*
Plods on to *Heaven;* and ne'er is at a loss:
For the *Streight-gate* wou'd be made *streighter* yet,
Were *none* admitted there but men of *Wit.*
The few, by Nature form'd, with Learning fraught,
Born to instruct, as others to be taught,
Must Study well the Sacred Page; and see
Which Doctrine, this, or that, does best agree
With the whole Tenour of the Work Divine:
And plainlyest points to Heaven's reveal'd Design:
Which Exposition flows from *genuine Sense;*
And which is *forc'd* by *Wit* and *Eloquence.*
(ll. 316-33)

Without any apparent doubt regarding Christ's divinity, these
verses reveal Dryden's failure, indeed his powerlessness, to
deny that even such passages in Scripture as those treating of
Christ's nature are susceptible of more than one meaning—this
in spite of Dryden's repeated claim that Scripture "In all things
needfull to be *known,* is *plain.*" In shifting the grounds of the

discussion from the particular question posed to the quite different and broader claim that a limited core of belief is essential for salvation, Dryden reveals that for him Scripture alone is not able, after all, to settle all necessary questions and cannot, therefore, serve as the desired final judge and authority.

Other swerves occur as a result of the play of figurative language—precisely what Dryden wanted to avoid. The desire to avoid the emotional intensity and the falsifying of figurative language, which is widely thematized in the Restoration (and elsewhere), is, of course, impossible. The desire itself, far from negligible, may be self-subverting, revealing the absence of nonfigurative language: one cannot "desire that with which one coincides." Thus the starting point is the *desire* of nonfigurative language, that is, the *lack* of nonfigurative language.[8]

It seems, moreover, that Dryden can only be indirect and figurative in describing the *"Letter"* and the supposed directness of God. That is, in spite of his desire and his expressed intention, Dryden writes figuratively about the putative plainness of Scripture, swerving from the desired literalness that supposedly characterizes the Bible. One brief passage will establish the point. After arguing that the written word is more reliable than the voice of (Catholic) tradition, itself said to be fundamentally implicated in error, Dryden reverts to the privileging of voice, which Derrida labels "phonocentrism," characteristic of the Western mind. According to Derrida, the voice is a sign of immediacy and presence, which is, of course, also signaled in the desire for the literal. Dryden writes, indeed, as we have already noted, that Scripture *"speaks* it *Self."* He thus tropes, turns, swerves, using the very figurative language he has sought to avoid. Though literalness is one of Dryden's major desiderata, and standards, in *Religio Laici,* his text cannot signify literally but only metaphorically, and so subject and mode are not mutually expressive. If the above is an accurate account of Dryden's text, declared intentions being subverted by his language, what happens to the truth-claims of the master

master-text, God's *"Will produc'd,"* even that name for which is a metaphor?

In any case, the power of figurative language is everywhere present in *Religio Laici,* and Dryden is powerless to *control* it —which is not to say either that another, perhaps more skillful writer *could* control it or that Dryden is the simple slave of language. The ceaseless play of language may be approached in several ways. As Paul de Man has taught us, the power of figurative language can be read in even an apparently innocuous rhetorical question. De Man cites the example of Archie Bunker being asked by his wife Edith (the dingbat) whether he wants his bowling shoes laced over or laced under, to which Archie responds with the question "What's the difference?" As de Man writes, that question "did not ask for difference but means instead 'I don't give a damn what the difference is.' The same grammatical pattern engenders two meanings that are mutually exclusive: the literal meaning asks for the concept (difference) whose existence is denied by the figurative meaning."[9] One could easily enough show the power of the rhetorical question in, for example, Yeats's "How can we know the dancer from the dance?" (as de Man does) or in the frequent recurrence of Archie Bunker's question in *Madame Bovary* (as I hope to do elsewhere).

Consider now what happens in *Religio Laici* as a result of a rhetorical question. The passage I refer to ostensibly participates in the poem's thematic development and purposive movement, which takes the reader from a sense of imagined self-sufficiency to complete reliance on God. Dryden writes: "How can the *less* the *Greater* comprehend? / Or *finite Reason* reach *Infinity?* / For what cou'd *Fathom GOD* were *more* than *He"* (ll. 39-41). At stake is nothing less than the relation between God and man, which has occasioned Dryden's entire effort.

As rhetorical questions, the first two lines I quoted have both literal and figurative meanings. Rather than different perspectives that may ultimately be reconcilable, these meanings appear mutually exclusive. The figurative meaning of the rhetorical questions does not ask for a positive response, one that would detail the specific ways in which "the *less*" could comprehend "the *Greater.*" The figurative meaning, instead, asserts that man *cannot* comprehend God and that it is, in fact, foolhardy even to ask the question since *"finite Reason"* obviously cannot "reach *Infinity.*" But the literal meaning of the lines insists on an answer, one that would deny the assertion of the figurative, describing the ways in which man can come to comprehend God.

At stake here is not one or two lines but the entire poem, for "two entirely coherent but entirely incompatible readings" of *Religio Laici* hinge on these lines, "whose grammatical structure is devoid of ambiguity, but whose rhetorical mode turns the mood as well as the mode of the entire poem upside down."[10] Certainly, one may read *Religio Laici,* as I have done above (and elsewhere), as an eloquent declaration of man's need to rely completely, in faith, on God, from whom he is so far distanced as to be unable to comprehend Him or His (to man's limited understanding) inscrutable ways. But the literal meaning of line 39, at least, undoes that entire scheme. Indeed, each detail of the poem may be read as supporting the divergent interpretation that man *can* come to comprehend "the *Greater.*" The key here would be the idea that man comprehends God insofar as He has chosen to reveal Himself through the mediation of Scripture, and that point apparently finds expression in such lines as the following:

Vain, wretched Creature, how art thou misled
To think thy Wit these God-like Notions bred!
These Truths are not the product of thy Mind,
But dropt from Heaven, and of a Nobler kind.
Reveal'd Religion first inform'd thy Sight,
And *Reason* saw not, till *Faith* sprung the Light.

> Hence all thy *Natural Worship* takes the *Source:*
> 'Tis *Revelation* what thou thinkst *Discourse.*
>
> (ll. 64-71)

But if man can comprehend God, even if the means be a gift from God Himself, then man is hardly so distanced from Him as Dryden has suggested, and finite reason has at the very least approached the Infinite.

Yet the figurative meaning of the questions in lines 39-40 makes it impossible to decide that this interpretation of the poem is preferable. The lines I quoted above can just as easily be read as a definite indication of the unbridgeable distance (and difference) between man and God. What de Man writes about Yeats's "Among School Children" is thus applicable to a large extent to *Religio Laici:* "The two readings . . . engage each other in direct confrontation, for the one reading is precisely the error denounced by the other and has to be undone by it. Nor can we in any way make a valid decision as to which of the readings can be given priority over the other; none can exist in the other's absence."[11] *Religio Laici* thus maintains that man can and cannot fathom God. Who, then, is master, or, better, what is the precise relation between man and God?

Perhaps we can reach, if not an answer, at least a better understanding of the question by continuing our reading of line 39, in which the syntax complicates considerably the rhetoric. Indeed, the syntax produces two quite different readings (much as grammar produces two different readings of such lines as "*God*'s Word they had not, but the *Priests* they had"): in addition to the reading I have been assuming (how can man comprehend God?), there is the possibility the line asks how God can comprehend man. Not a likely reading, admittedly, though it acquires some cogency when we note that the verb "comprehend" means to take in, embrace, include, as well as to understand. In any case, this second meaning of the verb complicates even further the meaning of line 39, for, assuming at least for the moment that the syntax is to be understood in the more likely way, the line would be seen as asking how "the *less*" can include "the *Greater.*" This meaning of the verb could, then, join with a literal meaning of the rhetorical question in putting in doubt any absolute distinction between man and God—or slave and master or even reader and text. Though Dryden declares that if man can fathom God, he is then more than God, his poem describes a situation of mutual need and dependency. The point is significantly strengthened in that Dryden uses the comparative degree in the line, referring to God as "the *Greater,*" to man as "the *less.*" This usage interimplicates man and God, for as described neither can exist in the other's absence.

If God cannot be thought apart from man, and vice versa, then, to return to the question on which we noted a swerve, what of Christ? He is evidently the God-man, but then so is every other human being, each of whom carries a "trace" of God, who carries a "trace" of man. In a radical sense, the space separating God and man is bridged, the Gospel being the good news, as Nietzsche wrote, that there are no more opposites.[12]

There no longer appears an ontological absolute authority distinct from man to which man must subject himself. The hierarchy Dryden seeks to preserve breaks down; indeed, hierarchization breaks down. But that effect results not from Dryden's named opponents who would dethrone God and install man in His place but from the play of language which shows God and man to be inextricably related to each other, the "center," as it were, including in "itself" the margin and so being originarily decentered and not "itself."

Likewise *Religio Laici:* it is heterogeneous, dialogical, bifurcated, different from "itself," for what the text describes differs from, indeed wars with, what it declares. As a consideration of its concepts, figures, and the relation between them makes clear, the poem contains mutually exclusive meanings. It is

therefore unreadable in the sense that no complete understanding, no fully present comprehension is possible. *Religio
Laici* is the story of the wandering of its meaning. The Bible,
the story of the wandering of the People of the Book, must be
similarly unreadable: it can be no more direct and unswerving
than Dryden's own text. Figuration, or swerving, subverts declared meanings, and so reading as commonly understood
plainly is made both impossible and possible.

7. Allegory of Blindness and Insight:

Will and Will-ing in *A Tale of a Tub*

Whatever reader desires to have a thorough comprehension of an author's thoughts, cannot take a better method, than by putting himself into the circumstances and postures of life, that the writer was in upon every important passage as it flowed from his pen, for this will introduce a parity and strict correspondence of ideas between the reader and the author. (p. 265)

They will furnish plenty of noble matter for such, whose converting imaginations dispose them to reduce all things into types; who can make shadows, no thanks to the sun, and then mould them into substances, no thanks to philosophy; whose peculiar talent lies in fixing tropes and allegories to the letter, and refining what is literal into figure and mystery. (p. 342)

The true illuminated (that is to say, the darkest of all) have met with such numberless commentators, whose scholastic midwifery hath delivered them of meanings, that the authors themselves perhaps never conceived,

and yet may very justly be allowed the lawful parents of
them, the words of such writers being like seed, which,
however scattered at random, when they light upon a
fruitful ground, will multiply far beyond either the hopes or
imagination of the sower. (pp. 339–40)

Whatever difference may be found in [commentators']
several conjectures, they will be all, without the least
distortion, manifestly deducible from the text. (p. 339)[1]

These passages from throughout *A Tale of a Tub* illustrate
a number of its characteristic features, including its complexity
and sophistication and its central thematic concern with reading and interpretation.[2] They also suggest some of the ways in
which this strange and discomfiting *écriture* ("book" hardly
seems appropriate, though "text" will perhaps do, for it is often
impossible to decide who is writing here) resembles and anticipates several recent critical and theoretical positions. The first
example I provided bears a striking affinity with the so-called
criticism of consciousness of such "Geneva critics" as
Georges Poulet, which has also been called "the tradition of
identity."[3] Indicative of the (mis)readings of their father's will in
the Allegory of the Coats and the Three Brothers, my second
example reminds one of both Harold Bloom's willful mispri-
sions and the recent fascination, in structuralism and deconstruction alike, with rhetoric understood as the study of tropes.
If a similar parallel suggests itself in my last example, the third
one anticipates both Geoffrey Hartman's general call to return
to allegoresis and exegetical modes of interpretation and his
specific advice on "how to reap a page" in *Saving the
Text.*[4]

Even apart from these striking echoes, which tempt one to
a metaleptical reversal of influence, thinking of the *Tale* as
repeating what has recently been written, this puzzling and
amazing text sounds themes now popular and often valorized.
For example, when the *Tale* admits that "how to analyze the

tub, was a matter of difficulty" (p. 263), we are likely to read this as the self-reflexivity now often prized in "primary" and "secondary" texts alike as well as a direct reference to the Hack's attempt to deflect the "grandees of Church and State" from "pick[ing] holes in the weak sides of Religion and Government" (ibid.). Moreover, the *Tale's* frequent contradictions of itself, or at least the Hack's contradictions of himself, will immediately suggest to the reader familiar with deconstruction "the critical difference" that is inevitable in all texts, made of language and so bifurcated and dialogical.[5]

But if those given to "hermeneutical highjinks"[6] are quick to value *A Tale of a Tub* as prescient and insightful, indeed as deconstructing the idea of the book as a totality, a more traditional critic will just as quickly object that these supposed insights are being satirized. Rather than Swift's own points, they are evidently part of the madness characteristic of the Hack, who intimates that his own imagination is "exceedingly disposed to run away with his reason . . . upon which account, my friends will never trust me alone, without a solemn promise to vent my speculations in this, or the like manner, for the universal benefit of human kind" (p. 336). A deconstructionist like Paul de Man might retort, however, that Swift is of course blind to such insights as my opening quotations provide, his text precisely being most insightful in those areas in which the "mad" Hack is most vigorously satirized.[7] Yet, because it ridicules such textual difference as deconstructive readings produce, *A Tale of a Tub* may complicate de Man's well-known account of the play of textual blindness and insight. Still, by means of close attention to both its declaration and its description of author-reader relations, I shall argue that the *Tale* is precisely an allegory of blindness and insight, telling the story of their crossing.

Though the *Tale* is frequently read as a satire on Modern writing, the Hack being, for example, unable to adhere to "what is to the purpose" (p. 317), ultimately admitting, in fact, that he is "now trying an experiment very frequent among modern authors; which is to write upon *Nothing;* when the subject is utterly exhausted, to let the pen still move on" (p. 352), it is principally concerned with abuses in reading. Linking the satire on the "numerous and gross corruptions in Religion and Learning" (p. 243) and so the Allegory of the Coats and the Three Brothers with the digressions, in fact, is interpretation, the main issue treated in both "parts" of the *Tale.* The *Tale* thus participates in that important but little-studied Augustan interest in reading and interpretation that Dryden makes the center of attention in *Religio Laici,* which can be read as a layman's approach to reading. The *Tale* may even be "about" the effort to read and a satire on the perhaps inevitable desire to reduce and make comprehensible.[8]

In certain respects, the positions of Swift and his cousin Dryden are similar, even though the latter is lashed in the *Tale:* both worry about the disturbing and disrupting power of figurative language, and both desire as a supposed bulwark against figurality an unthreatening literalness. As we have seen, Swift opposes "the converting imagination," which "fix[es] tropes and allegories to the letter, and refin[es] what is literal into figure and mystery." Those who thus give rein to the fancy are among those who "have spiritualized and refined [their writings] from the dross and grossness of sense and human reason" (p. 274). Because then—so the argument goes—Swift values reason, "the senses, and common understanding," which leads one to pass his "life in the common forms" (p. 331), he prefers the plain, literal sense, as in the father's directions concerning his will (about which more shortly) to the allegorical and "mythological" readings produced by "the converting imagination." Incidentally, this valorization of literal readings interestingly coincides with Swift's frequent literalizing of metaphors; characteristic of his writing generally, literalizing occurs in the *Tale* when, for example, Peter is said to value most "a certain set of bulls" (p. 300; the reference is of course to Papal bulls), when the Hack describes his "dissect[ion of] the carcass of human nature" (p. 307), and when the Hack expatiates on his "histori-theo-physi-logical account of zeal, showing how it first proceeded from a notion into a word, and from thence in a hot summer ripened into a tangible substance" (p. 314). Common to Swift's preference of the literal and his frequent literalizing of metaphors is de-mystification.

But unlike Dryden, who believes that Scripture at least is so plain and clear as to require no interpretation, Swift nowhere in the *Tale* suggests any hope that plain and clear language will yield unequivocal meaning. Rather, he focuses on the ways by which even supposedly plain meanings are abused, converted, and willfully misread. Well aware of how texts can be, and frequently are, mauled and used for one's own purposes, Swift urges final recourse to authorial intention. He makes the point forcefully in the "Apology" (for example, pp. 248, 253) and repeats it, generalized, as in the note on p. 340: "Nothing is more frequent than for commentators to force interpretation, which the author never meant."

The point emerges most clearly in the Allegory of the Coats and the Three Brothers (writing an allegory, Swift obviously distinguishes between allegorized reading and the reading of allegory[9]). "Once upon a time," the story begins, there was a certain man with three sons, who on his deathbed bequeathed to them three coats, along with his will containing "full instructions in every particular concerning the wearing and management of your coats" and commanding that they "live together in one house like brethren and friends" (pp. 280-81). Though the brothers soon fall out with each other in a dispute over the will, it is plain and clear. According to the Hack, "it consisted," in fact, "wholly in certain plain, easy directions about the management and wearing of their coats, with legacies and penalties, in case of obedience or neglect" (p. 342). Influenced by Peter, the well-read brother familiar with Aristotle's *de Interpretatione* (p. 286), the brothers find it possible, because desirable, to read into and out of the will whatever they decide upon. For one example of Peter's willful misreading, consider the following passage, which describes the brothers' allegorizing in order to authorize their desire for the expressly forbidden silver fringe:

> "*Item,* I charge and command my said three sons to wear no sort of silver fringe upon or about their said coats," etc., with a penalty in case of disobedience, too long here to insert. However, after some pause the brother so often mentioned for his erudition, who was well skilled in criticisms, had found in a certain author, which he said should be nameless, that the same word which in the will is called fringe, does also signify a broom-stick, and doubtless ought to have the same interpretation in this paragraph. This, another of the brothers disliked, because of that epithet silver, which could not, he humbly conceived, in propriety of speech be reasonably applied to a broom-stick; but it was replied upon him, that this epithet was understood in a mythological and allegorical sense. However, he objected again, why their father should forbid them to wear a broom-stick on their coats, a caution that seemed unnatural and impertinent; upon which he was taken up short, as one that spoke irreverently of a mystery, which doubtless was very useful and significant, but ought not to be over-curiously pried into, or nicely reasoned upon. And in short, their father's authority being now considerably sunk, this expedient was allowed to serve as a lawful dispensation for wearing their full proportion of silver fringe. (p. 288)

Later, Peter's interpretive authority having been questioned and the other two brothers having gained complete access to the will, Jack, not so different from his learned brother after all, "began to entertain a fancy that the matter was deeper and darker, and therefore must needs have a great deal more of mystery at the bottom" (p. 342). He sets out, therefore, to "prove this very skin of parchment to be meat, drink, and cloth, to be the philosopher's stone, and the universal medicine" (ibid.). Having decided beforehand that the will is not what it plainly is, Jack finds it easy, as Peter did, to make that will into whatever he wills: "He had a way of working it into any shape he pleased; so that it served him for a nightcap when he went to bed, and for an umbrella in rainy weather."

That the text at the center of this critical maelstrom is a will is another literalization of a metaphor and, I suggest, an example of Swift's insight (Dryden, as we saw, uses the same metaphor in *Religio Laici*); Swift's *Tale* literalizes the universal situation I described in "The Story of Error" as "a dialogue of questions that is a mutual coercion." Indeed, in the Allegory of the Coats and the Three Brothers, between the father, on the one hand, and the three sons, on the other, and then later among the sons themselves occurs a battle of wills, and that representation becomes an allegory of the will and the will-ing involved in the reading of any text. Every textual field is, in fact, constituted as a battle of wills, claims of authority, and the force of desire. In Swift's Allegory, the text left to the sons is a will —in more than one sense—imposed by the authority of the father in an effort to coerce them to do what he desires; even after he leaves them, he *wills* to exercise authority over them. But the sons, like all other readers, have wills and desires of their own, and so the battle is joined. Another way to put this perhaps, as I suggested in the two previous chapters, is to say that we witness in the Allegory a typical opposition between master and slave, authority being at stake. The father wills to be master, but the sons resist the slavery his authority would impose, restricting them to following the letter of his law, that is, to a simple execution of his "plain and easy directions." As happens whenever such oppositions exist, first one and then the other side gains the upper hand, the slave eventually be-

coming master and repeating the tyranny. It is not long, therefore, before "their father's authority" is "considerably sunk."
Of course, the *desire* of mastery, no matter in whom, represents precisely the *lack* of mastery, for "it is not possible to
desire that with which one coincides."[10] To modify a well-
known Derridean point, "Without the possibility of difference,
the desire of [mastery] as such would not find its breathing-
space." According to Derrida, that means that "this desire
carries in itself the destiny of its non-satisfaction. Difference
produces what it forbids, makes possible the very thing that it
makes impossible."[11] If this begins to sound like the Hack's
subversion of logic, that may be just the point.

Swift, of course, sides with the father, or the author, in this
agonistic struggle for author-ity. Indeed, in terms of interpretive
strategy, the reader, says Swift, should always seek the intentions—or authority—of the author in his quest to understand a
text. Reading becomes, then, exactly that effort to achieve
coincidence or harmony that is expressed, though in perhaps
exaggerated fashion, in one of the quotations from the *Tale* I
used as an epigraph: "Whatever reader desires to have a
thorough comprehension of an author's thoughts, cannot take
a better method, than by putting himself into the circumstances
and postures of life, that the writer was in upon every important
passage as it flowed from his pen, for this will introduce a parity
and strict correspondence of ideas between the reader and the
author" (p. 265). Presented satirically, this passage nevertheless emerges as at least close to Swift's own desire that the
reader seek and then adhere to authorial intention. But, it
should be noted, the point concerning parity is misleading, for
the reader is here being advised to submit himself or herself
totally to the author, denying himself totally, emptying himself,
as he occupies another's space, body, and mind.

A Tale of a Tub thus focuses on the relation of author and
reader, insisting on the former's authority and pointing to the
dangers when the reader "usurps" that authority. So far, how-

ever, we have read only a part of the story the *Tale* tells, having attended to the text's declarations. We must try to be as rigorous as the text and so should attend as well to its figurative language. We have already seen, of course, that the *Tale* is built, despite Swift's preference for the literal, on word play: there is the play not only on will but also on author and authority.[12]

The *Tale* provides a chain of passages perhaps continuing this play of words (and sounds) but certainly relating writing to riding. Begin with this passage, which opens Section XI: "in writing it is as in travelling: if a man is in haste to be at home . . . if his horse be tired with long riding and ill ways, or be naturally a jade, I advise him clearly to make the straightest and the commonest road, be it ever so dirty. But then surely we must own such a man to be a scurvy companion at best" (p. 341). Other passages also employ the rider/horse analogy. First, a passage comparing the relationship of mind to its thoughts with that of rider to horse: "And whereas the mind of Man, when he gives the spur and bridle to his thoughts, doth never stop, but naturally sallies out into both extremes of high and low, of good and evil; his first flight of fancy commonly transports him to ideas of what is most perfect, finished, and exalted" (p. 324). Second, a passage presenting the relationship of reason to imagination as analogous to that of rider to horse: "I myself . . . am a person, whose imaginations are hard-mouthed, and exceedingly disposed to run away with his reason, which I have observed from long experience to be a very light rider, and easily shook off" (p. 336). Third, the well-known passage that continues at least the imagery of mounting but inverts the (proper) relationship described in the previous quotation: "But when a man's fancy gets astride on his reason, when imagination is at cuffs with the senses, and common understanding, as well as common sense, is kicked out of doors, the first proselyte he makes is himself" (p. 331). By means of the figures employed, Swift rigorously argues that the mind and the reason must not allow its thoughts and the imagination to have free rein, run away, and so usurp proper authority. Properly ordered, reason mounts and rides the imagination; madness occurs when that order is inverted and imagination takes the place of reason.

Now consider the following passage, in which the same figurative language we have been reading is used to present directly the relationship of reader to writer: "Among these last [handles for catching hold of mankind], curiosity is one, and of all others affords the firmest grasp: curiosity, that spur in the side, that bridle in the mouth, that ring in the nose, of a lazy and impatient and a grunting reader. By this handle it is, that an author should seize upon his readers; which as soon as he has once compassed, all resistance and struggling are in vain, and they become his prisoners as close as he pleases, till weariness or dullness force him to let go his grip" (p. 350). There is no question here of the reader-horse running away with the writer-rider or of taking his place. The passage says, however, that the writer should hold fast the reader by means of the latter's curiosity. It says something else: though the reader, like the fancy or the imagination or the thoughts, must be governed, the reader is essential. In the terms of the passage quoted, reading is being mounted; if it is an act of being controlled by the author, it is also that author's means of conveyance along the journey that is writing. Without the reader, then, the writer cannot move. The writer needs the reader. The relationship of writer to reader may be one of master to slave, but it is at least complicated by the situation of need it describes.

The language Swift employs to present the writer-reader relationship is, of course, sexual. In "mounting" the reader, the writer assumes the supposed sexual authority of the male, occupying the male's position in relation to the female position of the reader. The following passage, which opens with the paradoxical relationship of blindness to insight, raising again the question of Swift's own blindness and insight, explores most thoroughly the links among writer/reader, master/slave, and male/female:

> Wise philosophers hold all writings to be fruitful in the proportion they are dark; and therefore, the true illuminated (that is to say, the darkest of all) have met with such numberless commentators, whose scholastic midwifery hath delivered them of meanings, that the authors themselves perhaps never conceived, and yet may very justly be allowed the lawful parents of them, the words of such writers being like seed, which, however scattered at random, when they light upon a fruitful ground, will multiply far beyond either the hopes or imagination of the sower. (pp. 339-40)

We must read carefully this difficult passage. Though Swift desires that the natural parent have the authority, his language complicates the matter considerably. First, Swift concedes a good bit in turning immediately to the question of the "lawful," that is, the merely conventional or socially established. Moreover, his figures carry him well beyond, and indeed counter to, his apparent intentions, for as with the previous passage we read, the writer no longer appears as independent, autonomous authority. According to this passage, indeed, the writer-male sows his seed, which requires for growth and development the fertile ground that is the reader-female. In this situation of partnership described by Swift's figurative language, the reader is just as important as the writer, the mother as the father. But the passage directly confronts another, related, and more immediate point, and that concerns the relation among writer, words, and meanings. A note following the word "seed" in the passage claims that "nothing is more frequent than for commentators to force interpretation, which the author never meant." Likewise, the main passage asserts that commentary "delivers" texts of meanings "the authors themselves perhaps never conceived." That is, commentary is creative, bringing out of the text what the author never put in. Yet the passage proceeds to grant that, even so, the author is the lawful parent because words are like seed. Here the passage obscures the crucial distinction between the author as male sowing his sperm-seed and author as sower of words as seed. But if words are like seed, and not just the male seed, they are no longer within the author's range of authority and control. Though the male may be said to have authored another being, no matter how scattered his seed was, what authority can seed, or words, claim? Surely not that of the sower, whose function is minimal. If the author is, then, like the sower of seed, rather than a father, his authority regarding the words sown or their meanings is negligible. If this is true, then contrary to Swift's claim, interpretations are not forced: words being free, freeplay reigns. Parentage is thus questioned, and so is the authority of the author. What we have here is evidently an example of what the text itself calls "uncontrollable demonstration" (p. 260).[13]

In "A Digression concerning Critics" occurs another questioning of author-ity and a subversion of logic. According to the Hack, the Moderns "have proved beyond contradiction, that the very finest things *delivered* of old, have been long since invented, and brought to light by much later *pens;* and that the noblest discoveries those ancients ever made, of art or of nature, have all been produced by the transcending genius of the present age" (pp. 292-93, italics added). What was earlier delivered has recently been invented. The present has produced, that is, made, the discoveries past ages offered. The later pen (or penis) has authored what had been much earlier delivered. Is this satirized passage insightful or merely mad in its deconstruction of author-ity?

Logic is, of course, similarly flouted elsewhere in *A Tale of a Tub.* Homer, for example, that "tolerable genius," is blasted for his "many gross errors": not only did he "read but very superficially either Sendivogius, Behmen, or *Anthroposophia Theomagica,*" but—"a fault far more notorious to tax this author with"—Homer also reveals "gross ignorance in the common laws of this realm, and in the doctrine as well as discipline of the Church of England" (pp. 308-9). There is no denying the Hack's general madness, for as Swift presents him, his fancy has gotten astride his reason and has driven out the "common understanding."

We can now see, however, thanks especially to the work of Derrida, de Man, and others, that what the Hack says, though presented as madness by the satirist, contains much insight. As Barbara Johnson puts it, a deconstructive reading shows "the *necessity* with which what [an author] *does* see is systematically related to what he does *not* see."[14] In the Hack, as in Swift's own declarations, appears a complex mixture of blindness and insight, which complicates the usual binary opposition. The supposedly insightful (i.e., satirical) text may then appear most blind in condemning the blind but insightful Hack. *A Tale of a Tub* itself makes the point when the Hack comments upon "how near the frontiers of height and depth border upon each other," how "one who travels the east [eventually runs] into the west," and how "a straight line [is eventually] drawn by its own length into a circle" (pp. 324-25). Blindness and insight appear to relate to each other as do fancy and reason, slave and master, female and male, reader and writer, reading and writing. In this situation the will is a very complicated text.

8. "Grac[ing] These Ribalds":

The Play of Difference in Pope's *Epistle to Dr. Arbuthnot*

An Epistle to Dr. Arbuthnot is normally read as Pope's defense of himself and justification of his satire, as—in other words—his *apologia pro satura sua*. In the prose "Advertisement" that precedes the poem, Pope describes his aim, in fact, in legal terms as an indictment, establishing an adversarial situation and pitting himself and his word against certain others, their charges, and their "truth": "This Paper is a Sort of Bill of Complaint, begun many years since, and drawn up by snatches, as the several Occasions offer'd. I had no thoughts of publishing it, till it pleas'd some Persons of Rank and Fortune . . . to attack in a very extraordinary manner, not only my Writings (of which being publick the Publick judge) but my *Person, Morals,* and *Family,* whereof to those who know me not, a truer Information may be requisite."[1] After making clear his own desire to tell the truth, Pope proceeds to describe himself as "divided between the Necessity to say something of Myself, and my own Laziness to undertake so awkward a Task." This confession of self-division is perhaps more suggestive, and important, than has hitherto been recognized. These two kinds of difference, that external form consisting of difference between (say) Pope and those he indicts, and the internal form representing self-division and rendering certain conventions problematical, will be my focus here. I shall attend, that is, to the story told by the play of difference in *Arbuthnot.* My effort, hardly exhaustive, will be exploratory and speculative.

I begin with Pope's defense, which consists in large part of a series of strategies designed to establish him as a "good man." He differentiates, for example, his background, motives, and character from those of "the Race that write" (l. 219), maintaining that, unlike the "Clerk, foredoom'd his Father's soul to cross, / Who pens a Stanza when he should *engross"* (ll. 17-18), he "left no Calling for this idle trade, / No Duty broke, no Father dis-obey'd (ll. 129-30). Depicting himself as a good man, Pope claims to rise above the level of "slashing *Bentley"* and "piddling *Tibalds"* (l. 164), proceeding to adduce a list of illustrious friends to prove the difference; from them, he asserts, "the world will judge of Men and Books, / Not from the *Burnets, Oldmixons,* and *Cooks"* (ll. 145-46).

Pope focuses strategically on this matter of friendship as a means of establishing his virtue and his difference. Perhaps his most effective and economical rhetorical use of friendship appears in the choice of John Arbuthnot as "recipient" of his "epistle" and as interlocutor. As is well known, Pope draws on a tradition suggested in Ecclesiasticus 6:16 ("A faithful friend is the medicine of life") and developed by Plutarch, who, in a disquisition entitled "How to Know a Flatterer from a Friend," uses as a recurrent motif the comparison of a good friend to an able physician. Of course, Arbuthnot was by profession a physician (he had, in fact, been physician to Queen Anne), and if one accepts the view expressed by Sir William Temple, Pope is especially blessed in having a doctor as a friend: "In all Diseases of Body and Mind, 'tis happy to have an able Physician for a Friend, or a discreet friend for a Physician; which is so great a blessing that the Wise Man will have it to proceed only from God." [2] That Arbuthnot was a satirist as well as a

physician (he wrote the *History of John Bull,* coauthored with
Pope and Gay *Three Hours after Marriage,* and was a member
of the Scriblerus Club) allows Pope to suggest also the familiar
notion that the satirist is, despite appearances to the contrary,
a physician and a friend.[3] Finally, because Arbuthnot was
widely respected, Pope is able to draw on a tradition perhaps
deriving from Aristotle's *Ethics* and to suggest that his friendship with such a man evidences his own virtue.[4] When this
good man speaks in the poem as interlocutor, therefore, his
words carry considerable weight and authority. In his five short
"speeches," Arbuthnot urges caution and restraint, warning
against the naming of individuals (ll. 75-78, 101-4), but he
also assists in his friend's satire on Sporus (ll. 305-8).

The terms this particular friend enables Pope to exploit,
"physician," "satirist," and "friend," serve indeed as focal
structuring devices for the defense. The idea that links the first
two here, "friend" is also the concept that differs from while
connecting two other terms crucial to the poem's thematic
development and Pope's strategies of defense. The terms appear together in lines 206-7: "A tim'rous foe, and a suspicious
friend, / Dreading ev'n fools, by Flatterers besieg'd." Pope, of
course, opposes "friend" to "foe," and the other term, "flatterers," is both distinguished from and linked to "foes"; indeed,
the construction of line 104, which brings together the conclusion of Arbuthnot's warning concerning names and Pope's
response thereto, illustrates the similarity and difference of the
terms: " 'But Foes like these!'—One Flatt'rer's worse than all."
Pope's claims may, then, be described as follows: Because the
satirist is a physician of sorts, he is ultimately a friend, even of
those he lashes, intending to cure them of their follies and
vices: "This dreaded Sat'rist *Dennis* will confess / Foe to his
Pride, but Friend to his Distress" (ll. 370-71). A satirist obviously differs from a flatterer, who, Pope insists, is ultimately a
foe (Bufo well illustrates the point).

Though I have no doubt oversimplified in summarizing, the
above represents, I think, Pope's basic line of argument in *An*

Epistle to Dr. Arbuthnot. Indeed, Pope's defense exhibits many of the qualities Margaret W. Ferguson claims as characteristic of the tradition of defenses of poetry; being classifiable as neither disinterested art nor disinterested critical commentary, becoming in fact "active rather than passive advocates for what we might call the claims of the ego," these defenses, according to Ferguson, act as "protection against external threats to the ego's task of defending itself against internal threats." It is impossible to do justice here to Ferguson's subtle and complex argument, and I have no intention of trying to apply her arguments to *Arbuthnot* in any consistent way, though a certain parallel will emerge between my argument below and her claim that the usual poetic defense "involves a complex double movement of attack and courtship."[5] But of course, Pope's "Bill of Complaint" is more than merely defensive. To use J. Paul Hunter's helpful terms, in this poem satiric apology turns into satiric instance[6]—one of several turns we shall consider. From the very beginning, indeed, Pope is concerned to draw straight, distinct, and unmistakable lines between himself and those others.

The poem opens, of course, with Pope seeking shelter from the would-be poets who besiege him wherever he goes. In escaping into his own home, Pope signals the desire for physical distance that is itself a sign of his desire for literary and moral differentiation. Outside, he maintains, with the poetasters lunacy rages, from which he would sequester and protect himself. The immediate danger Pope fears is contamination or infection; thus he laments, "What *Drop* or *Nostrum* can this Plague remove?" (l. 29). This seemingly innocent metaphor, like all other figures, carries great weight, for the medical plague has become, as here, a metaphor for a social plague. Indeed, it functions as a "generic label for a variety of ills that . . . threaten or seem to threaten the very existence of social life."[7] In texts as divergent as *Oedipus Rex, Troilus and Cressida,* and Camus's 1948 novel, the plague acts as part of a thematic cluster that involves epidemic contamination and eventually the dissolving of differences. If Pope cannot cure the plague or be inoculated against it, he can at least reduce the possibility of infection by quaranteening himself and perhaps thus maintaining the difference that the plague threatens to collapse.

Pope preserves his difference not only by escaping from the "plague" but also by establishing his difference from others who, he argues, lack sufficient difference. The desire to differentiate himself takes several forms. Some of these we have already glimpsed, including the differences in background, motive, and character he draws between himself and "the Race that write." Naming is another basic means of differentiation, perhaps the simplest, and Pope indulges in naming the specific targets of his satire, despite Arbuthnot's warnings. Pope's most elaborate and effective means of differentiation, which happens to be his main offensive strategy, the famous linked portraits of Atticus, Bufo, and Sporus, is designed to advance the defensive strategy of establishing Pope as an alternative—indeed, as a true friend and a good man.

Before turning to these portraits, it is necessary to examine carefully Pope's desire for difference and the implications of his wish for clear and absolute distinctions. Such desire appears to be masculine, Pope wanting from the outset to establish what he later calls his "manly ways" (l. 337). To be a good man and a true friend is, according to Pope's strategy, to be distinct, to possess a clear identity—in short, to be different. Difference is the male quality, the presence of the penis. Pope's fear of the loss of difference may be seen, then, as fear of the loss of his maleness, or castration. It is the fear that he will become, in fact, what Sporus was turned into: an in-different male, a male who was castrated and then treated as a woman, "one vile Antithesis. / Amphibious Thing!" (ll. 325-26). In Pope's case, however, it is not so much castration as intercourse with him, feminized, that threatens: "What Walls can guard me, or what Shades can hide? / They pierce my Thickets, thro' my Grot they glide" (ll. 7-8). The judgment rendered by Pope, after being "Seiz'd and ty'd down to judge" (l. 33), certainly carries sexual overtones: " 'Keep your Piece nine years' " (l. 40), an imagined suitor's reaction to which extending the implication (" 'The Piece you think is incorrect: why take it, / I'm all submission, what you'd have it, make it,' " ll. 45-46). Feminized, Pope withdraws from these suitors and their assaults, declaring in the poem's opening lines, "Shut, shut the door, good *John!* fatigu'd I said, / Tye up the knocker, say I'm sick, I'm dead," "knocker" perhaps being the penis.

The enigmatic feminization, or attempted feminization, of Pope cannot be understood, I contend, apart from the metaphorical treatment of writing in *Arbuthnot.* Pope of course claims that, whereas for the "Witlings" writing is a compulsion and a drive akin to madness, for him it is both a burden and a moral obligation. He also treats writing in sexual terms, as when he notes that "ev'ry Coxcomb knows me by my *Style*" (l. 282) and when he counsels to " 'Keep your Piece nine years,' " "Piece" being both the written text and the sexual instrument and *"Style"* suggesting the *stylus* or penis. The references to Gildon's "venal quill" (l. 151), to Bufo "puff'd by ev'ry quill" (l. 232), and to "each gray goose quill" that a patron may bless (l. 249), as well as to "slashing *Bentley"* (l. 164), indicate the relation of pen to penis—writing, according to Freud, entailing "making a liquid flow out of a tube onto a piece of white paper" and so assuming "the significance of copulation."[8] The mob of would-be poets courting favor and Pope are thus said "To spread about the Itch of Verse and Praise" (l. 224). Pope makes clear that the writer with his pen(is) seeks pen-etration and satisfaction. As a result of Pope's own (masculine) writing, moreover, "Poor *Cornus* sees his frantic Wife elope, / And curses Wit, and Poetry, and *Pope"* (ll. 25-26).

Further, Pope depicts his own reception as a writer in terms that define writing as a masculine act and the response to a writer as feminine. Pope indeed describes his own writing in sexual terms ("The Muse but serv'd to ease some Friend, not Wife," l. 131), the suggestion of homosexuality being (anachronistically) supported by the statement that his friends "left me GAY" (l. 256). If writing and writers are masculine, and the response sought feminine, we can appreciate why Pope as would-be patron, courted for favor, is being treated as female. He becomes the sexual object pursued by the "Witlings."

Recalling the Freudian implications of eyes and sight, we can appreciate too the nature of Pope's withdrawal from the poet-suitors as he summarizes that withdrawal: "I sought no homage from the Race that write; / I kept, like *Asian* Monarchs, from their sight" (ll. 219-20). Withdrawing, Pope refuses to mingle with the poetasters. He thus rejects the role of woman they seek to impose upon him: he will not be turned into their lover, their host, their patron.

Pope attempts, then, to preserve his difference (phallus) in the face of the dunces' aim to make him a patron-woman who can satisfy their desires as writer-males. He preserves his difference not only by withdrawing but also by establishing clear and distinct difference from others. Pope's most effective strategies of differentiation, and his most strenuous attacks, occur in the portraits of Atticus, Bufo, and Sporus, in which the language of sexuality and the sexuality of language are unmistakable.

The first portrait is of Atticus, whom Pope lashes for his failure to achieve distinct identity:

    ... were there One whose fires
True Genius kindles, and fair Fame inspires,
Blest with each Talent and each Art to please,
And born to write, converse, and live with ease:
Shou'd such a man, too fond to rule alone,

Bear, like the *Turk,* no brother near the throne,
View him with scornful, yet with jealous eyes,
And hate for Arts that caus'd himself to rise;
Damn with faint praise, assent with civil leer,
And without sneering, teach the rest to sneer;
Willing to wound, and yet afraid to strike,
Just hint a fault, and hesitate dislike;
Alike reserv'd to blame, or to commend,
A tim'rous foe, and a suspicious friend,
Dreading ev'n fools, by Flatterers besieg'd,
And so obliging that he ne'er oblig'd;
Like *Cato,* give his little Senate laws,
And sit attentive to his own applause;
While Wits and Templers ev'ry sentence raise,
And wonder with a foolish face of praise.
Who but must laugh, if such a man there be?
Who would not weep, if *Atticus* were he!

(ll. 193-214)

Different from the manliness Pope praises, Atticus appears weak, indistinct, unwilling to take a definite stand. He accedes to flattery, and if he attacks, it is barely. Unable to be really different, Atticus is not sufficiently masculine. Lacking in confidence, he fears competition for "the throne" and indeed hates the very "Arts" by which he has "risen" to that place.

With the second portrait the situation is more complicated. From more than one perspective Bufo is the central portrait— and arguably the most important difference Pope establishes in *Arbuthnot.* Bufo's importance derives in part from his similarity to Pope, particularly as the poet appears early on in the poem, courted by the flattering dunces. Pope's aim, of course, is to claim essential difference in this situation of similarity, thereby differentiating himself as true friend from the false friend (and foe) that Bufo the patron is. The theme of the portrait thus concerns the relationship of flatterer and flattered or, to use analogous terms, host and parasite. Clearly, the plagues of poetasters surrounding Bufo, like "the Race that write" courting Pope, are parasites. But just as clearly the patron-flattered-host Bufo functions also as a flatterer-parasite on what initially appear to be parasite-poetasters: for if as host Bufo feeds the "undistinguish'd race" of "Wits," he is fed in turn by the very parasites he feeds, feeding on the parasites, changing places with them in a "see-saw between *that* and *this*" (l. 323), and so finally becoming identifiable as neither simply parasite nor host, flatterer nor flattered, but as both.

> Proud, as *Apollo* on his forked hill,
> Sate full-blown *Bufo,* puff'd by ev'ry quill;
> Fed with soft Dedication all day long,
> *Horace* and he went hand in hand in song.
> His Library, (where Busts of Poets dead
> And a true *Pindar* stood without a head)
> Receiv'd of Wits an undistinguish'd race,
> Who first his Judgment ask'd, and then a Place:
> Much they extoll'd his Pictures, much his Seat,
> And flatter'd ev'ry day, and some days eat:
> Till grown more frugal in his riper days,
> He pay'd some Bards with Port, and some with Praise,
> To some a dry Rehearsal was assign'd,
> And others (harder still) he pay'd in kind.
> *Dryden* alone (what wonder?) came not nigh,
> *Dryden* alone escap'd this judging eye:
> But still the Great have kindness in reserve,
> He help'd to bury whom he help'd to starve.
>
> (ll. 231-48)

The sexual language we have noted elsewhere in *Arbuthnot* appears here, too. For the portrait treats the relationship of male-female, as well as that of patron-poet and parasite-host. As the opening lines of the portrait indicate, what Pope feared does happen to a patron: "full blown" and "puff'd by ev'ry quill," Bufo becomes female in hosting the would-be poets. Yet he gets his revenge on the emasculating writers by becoming the castrated-castrating woman, for in his library (or womb) lie "dead" poets, including Pindar, who "stood without a head." Are these writers merely "spent"? Or is it that, feminized, Bufo feminizes, turning the masculine writer into a female if he is allowed to have his way? Perhaps it is both. With the male-female relationship, in any case, as with those others it treats, the Bufo portrait dramatizes the turning of one thing into another, destabilizing, indeed, differences usually arrested as distinct oppositions.

If Atticus is neither quite one thing nor fully another, neither adequately friend nor identifiably foe, Sporus is, more dramatically than Bufo, *both* one thing *and* another. According to one of the shrewdest commentators on the poem, Sporus is, therefore, "the very reverse of the divine reconciliation of opposites."[9] Assumed to represent John Lord Hervey, well known for effeminacy of both manner and appearance, Sporus is an "Antithesis" and an "Amphibious Thing," both male and female, oscillating "between *that* and *this*":

Yet let me flap this Bug with gilded wings,
This painted Child of Dirt that stinks and stings;
Whose Buzz the Witty and the Fair annoys,
Yet Wit ne'er tastes, and Beauty ne'er enjoys,
So well-bred Spaniels civilly delight
In mumbling of the Game they dare not bite.
Eternal Smiles his Emptiness betray,
As shallow streams run dimpling all the way.
Whether in florid Impotence he speaks,
And, as the Prompter breathes, the Puppet squeaks;
Or at the Ear of *Eve,* familiar Toad,
Half Froth, half Venom, spits himself abroad,
In Puns, or Politicks, or Tales, or Lyes,
Or Spite, or Smut, or Rymes, or Blasphemies.

His Wit all see-saw between *that* and *this,*
Now high, now low, now Master up, now Miss,
And he himself one vile Antithesis.
Amphibious Thing! that acting either Part,
The trifling Head, or the corrupted Heart!
Fop at the Toilet, Flatt'rer at the Board,
Now trips a Lady, and now struts a Lord.
Eve's Tempter thus the Rabbins have exprest,
A Cherub's face, a Reptile all the rest;
Beauty that shocks you, Parts that none will trust,
Wit that can creep, and Pride that licks the dust.

(ll. 309-33)

According to Aubrey Williams, the name "Sporus" derives from the youth that the emperor Nero caused to be castrated and then, treating him as a woman, eventually married.[10] Certainly, Pope's portrait presents Sporus as having lost his difference. He seems, in fact, to have succumbed, somewhat like Bufo, to pressures Pope has resisted, and that failure in Sporus no doubt accounts in part for the vigor of Pope's attack. Sporus both attacks and flatters, and so his efforts evidently cancel each other out. He is self-divided, opposing forces colliding within him. According to Pope, he is, then, impotent and empty.

Taking the portraits together, we notice a certain progression: whereas Atticus is not male enough, Bufo appears feminized, and Sporus is divided, being both male and female. The straight lines Pope has sought blur in Atticus, curve in Bufo, and become indeterminate, undecidable in Sporus. To them Pope aims to be an effective alternative, with his "manly ways." He has, of course, acted in an apparently "manly" way in setting up these differences in hopes of preserving his difference. Having established that difference, in part by showing his difference from those lacking difference, Pope now exhibits some interesting differences from himself, at least from himself as he has appeared in the poem.

Though they are by no means radical breaks, important differences appear immediately following the Sporus portrait. To begin with, there is the change to third-person narration, indicative of the indirectness that replaces the directness we have noted. The accompanying change in tone is also marked, Pope now appearing patient and long-suffering, receiving rather than giving blows and apparently no longer so intent on the kind of differentiation evident earlier. For "Virtue's better end" (l. 342), he claims, he withstood

> The distant Threats of Vengeance on his head,
> The Blow unfelt, the Tear he never shed;
> The Tale reviv'd, the Lye so oft o'erthrown;
> Th' imputed Trash, and Dulness not his own;
> The Morals blacken'd when the Writings scape;
> The libel'd Person, and the pictur'd Shape;
> Abuse on all he lov'd, or lov'd him, spread,
> A Friend in Exile, or a Father, dead.
>
> (ll. 348-55)

Two verse paragraphs later Pope extends the argument, maintaining that he has actually befriended his attackers:

> Full ten years slander'd, did he once reply?
> Three thousand Suns went down on *Welsted*'s Lye:
> To please a *Mistress,* One aspers'd his life;
> He lash'd him not, but let her be his *Wife:*
> Let *Budgel* charge low *Grubstreet* on his quill,
> And write whate'er he pleas'd, except his *Will;*
> Let the *Two Curls* of Town and Court, abuse
> His Father, Mother, Body, Soul, and Muse.
>
> (ll. 374-81)

The shift in these paragraphs in tone and from first- to third-person are but two of several significant internal differences that the remainder of the poem develops. To continue, the verse paragraph from which I have just quoted closes with Pope's praise of his father and mother for their tolerance and forbearance—qualities the son has not displayed, at least through the Sporus passage. Whereas the poet passed judgment, assigned blame, and launched often-scathing attacks, his "Father held it for a rule / It was a Sin to call our Neighbour Fool, / That harmless Mother thought no Wife a Whore" (ll. 382-84). Obviously, such passages are designed to show the injustice of the attacks on Pope's family, but I think more is going on. For one thing, the following portrait of Pope's deceased father develops the differences between father and son, offering, indeed, a clear criticism of the poet as he appeared earlier in the poem. Presented as a kind of hero, the elder Pope is given the name the poet had sought for himself: "The good Man" (l. 395). Hero and *vir bonus,* the father is yet a *naif:* unlike his son, he was never involved in civil or religious controversy and never offered such a "Bill of Complaint" as is *An Epistle to Dr. Arbuthnot.* In phrases that inevitably recall his earlier depiction of "this long Disease, my Life" (l. 132), Pope even contrasts his father's lifelong healthfulness with his own illness and physical deformities:

> Born to no Pride, inheriting no Strife,
> Nor marrying Discord in a Noble Wife,
> Stranger to Civil and Religious Rage,
> The good Man walk'd innoxious thro' his Age.
> No Courts he saw, no Suits would ever try,
> Nor dar'd an Oath, nor hazarded a Lye:
> Un-learn'd, he knew no Schoolman's subtle Art,
> No Language, but the Language of the Heart.
> By Nature honest, by Experience wise,
> Healthy by Temp'rance and by Exercise:
> His Life, tho' long, to sickness past unknown,
> His Death was instant, and without a groan.
> (ll. 392-402)

Pope proceeds to pray that he be allowed to live and die like his father; if so, "Who sprung from Kings shall know less joy than I" (ll. 404-5). His father thus represents for Pope simplicity, naturalness, and innocence of discord, strife, and rage—in short, the pastoralism that the poet supposedly forsook as "not in Fancy's Maze he wander'd long, / But stoop'd to Truth, and moraliz'd his song" (ll. 340-41). Whether Pope now wishes to return to "Fancy's Maze," there appears a nostalgic longing for simplicity and escape that connects with the desire evidenced in the poem's opening to get away from the "plague" of poetasters. Though he sought to appear "the good man," Pope now appears different from "the good man." What does this say about his effort to establish and preserve his difference?

We approach an answer to that question by noting that Pope seems desirous of leaving behind the burden of writing, a masculine activity that is in the poem, as we have seen, aggressive, differentiating, and indeed divisive. In deemphasizing writing, Pope seems to put penis, as well as pen, away, for very little sexual language appears in later sections of *Arbuthnot.* Withdrawing from writing-sex, Pope, "sick of Fops, and Poetry, and Prate, / To *Bufo* left the whole *Castalian* State" (ll. 229-30). Having done so, he turns to his surviving but aged mother. Despite his earlier resistance to the attempted feminization of him, as well as his determined insistence on his "manly ways," Pope now depicts himself as nurse and mother to her. In effect, he changes places with his mother:

> Me, let the tender Office long engage
> To rock the Cradle of reposing Age,
> With lenient Arts extend a Mother's breath,
> Make Languor smile, and smooth the Bed of Death,
> Explore the Thought, explain the asking Eye,
> And keep a while one Parent from the Sky!
> (ll. 408-13)

At poem's end, then, Pope evidently rejects the divisive life of writing for the immediacy, naturalness, and supposed peace of home and family. Pope thus withdraws, adopting his father as model and ideal and apparently hoping to repeat the innocence he represents. In so doing, Pope completes, it seems, the pattern established at the opening of the poem. But much more is happening, as we have begun to see. In several ways Pope comes to differ from "himself," appearing divided, just as his poem does. Pope implicitly admits that his desire of difference has produced precisely difference from at least one major ideal and goal. Moreover, shortly after adopting his father as ideal, Pope—in a quite different sense—adopts his mother, indeed mothering her; though his father is an ideal (even if nonassertive, nondifferentiating, and so only problematically masculine), Pope becomes a mother. If this is so, if difference thus plays with our desire, what difference does the desire of difference make in those oppositions around which *Arbuthnot* is constructed?

It begins to appear that binary oppositions are illusory. Consider, for instance, Pope's desire all along to project "manly ways" and to resist the feminization apparent in the poetasters' efforts to make him their patron. In spite of himself, Pope reveals throughout certain supposedly feminine traits. For as he defends his hard-hitting truth-telling, Pope resembles a coquette: he asks, coyly, "You think this cruel?" (l. 83) and "Whom have I hurt?" (l. 95). Further, when he admits, "If wrong, I smil'd; if right, I kiss'd the rod" (l. 158), the *double entendre* establishes his own position as female. Moreover, the act of withdrawing, apparent in the opening couplet and culminating in Pope's focus at poem's end, seems a feminine act. Pope not only withdraws, of course, but, as we have seen, he also becomes nurse and mother. Thus differentiating, a masculine act, and withdrawing, a feminine one, result in the same loss of difference and the turn into the femininity Pope sought to avoid.

But "turn" can be misleading if it suggests a change from one stable and absolute identity into another. "Oscillation" may be better, for even when female qualities seem most apparent in Pope, they exist alongside and in oscillation with masculine ones. There are no absolute differences—and so no radical breaks in *Arbuthnot* before and after the Sporus portrait. Thus, even as he adopts his father as (nonassertive and nondifferentiating) model and ideal, Pope continues the (masculine) desire of clear, straight lines, for he posits his father as an absolute: innocent, simple, and natural. Pope thus substitutes one kind of absolute, one kind of distinctiveness, for another.

It seems that male and female qualities are actually coterminous in Pope as appears at poem's end when he is both drawn to his father and acts as mother. This is, of course, precisely what Pope objected to (and perhaps feared) in Sporus especially. It is to the Sporus portrait that I want now, in concluding, to return.

The internal split within the antithetical Sporus is obvious, but what that self-division signifies—and implies for Pope's own situation—may not be. Does it spell emptiness and impotence, as Pope declares? To begin with, consider that the name "Sporus" also suggests "spore," which comes from the New Latin *spora* (seed, spore), which derives from the Greek sense of both seed and the act of sowing, itself traceable to the word *speirein,* meaning "to sow." A spore is "a primitive usually unicellular resistant or reproductive body produced by plants and some invertebrates and capable of development into a new individual in some cases unlike the parent either directly or after fusion with another spore" *(Webster's New Collegiate Dictionary).* Whereas Sporus as a historical reference suggests the doubleness Pope emphasizes in the portrait, the etymology of the word denotes fertility and productiveness. This second, positive meaning is always in the word as a shimmering or trace that prevents the meaning from lying still or being unequivocal.

Though we may insist, with Pope, on Sporus' impotence, we can also insist on his at least potential fertility. That potential may, in fact, be seen as realized in Pope's satire. For within the poem the fertility is no longer merely potential but manifest and productive of satire. In a sense, Pope places Sporus, though not unproblematically, in the role of male to Pope's own female ability to produce.

The negative side of the coin that is Sporus, which represents Pope's declaration of Sporus' lack of difference as impotence, is simply but half the story. The other side shows how an internal split, an oscillation "between *that* and *this,*" can be positive and productive. The self-division satirized in Sporus is an analogue of, among other things, the internal split in Pope's poem between the (negative) declaration concerning Sporus and the (positive) description that has emerged through our reading. There are other internal splits, as we have seen, both Pope and his poem being fissured and self-divided, oscillating, just like Sporus, "between *that* and *this.*" Produced in each of these cases is a "both/and" situation, a dividing that is also a joining. If identities are thereby nullified, so are absolute differences. Left are relations, made possible by the "trace" of the "one" in the "other." The structure thus revealed "allows an osmotic mixing, making the stranger friend, the distant near, the *Unheimlich heimlich* . . . without, for all its closeness and similarity, ceasing to be strange, distant, and dissimilar."[11] Absolute difference such as Pope sought, we can now understand, must result in loss of difference; only relation preserves difference. Strangely, it seems, Sporus is the truth that Pope denies. The textual situation of undecidability between Sporus as potential and as impotent emerges, then, as an analogue, like the "trace-structure" of the word "Sporus," of the "both/and" nature Pope (satirically) ascribes to him. Is Sporus the "trace-structure"? In any case, instead of a vigorously masculine activity, writing emerges as another name for the "trace-structure" and for the modes of self-division *Arbuthnot* presents and enacts.

If an "uncanny antithetical relationship," resulting from inevitable internal fissure, thus "reforms itself in each polar opposite when that opposite is separated out," subverting or nullifying "the apparent unequivocal relation of polarity,"[12] then Pope's relationship to the mob of would-be poets, as well as to Atticus, Bufo, and Sporus, is rendered problematical. Unwilling patron, Pope is nonetheless host to the parasites (and therefore feminine) in at least the sense that they "live" inside his poem, taking life from it and being preserved in it, a point Pope himself suggests when he writes, "Ev'n such small Critics some regard may claim, / Preserv'd in *Milton*'s or in *Shakespeare*'s name" (ll. 167-68). Thus "the *Burnets, Oldmixons,* and *Cooks,*" as well as Atticus, Bufo, and Sporus, are given life by Pope even as he "destroys" them. There appears to be no undoing, or satirizing, that is not also a preserving. A similarly oscillating relationship obtaining between host and parasite, it is impossible to decide whether Sporus, for example, is the parasite within the host-text that is Pope's poem or the host on which that text feeds. Like Bufo, who is fed by his parasite-hosts, Pope himself can be seen as perhaps not much less parasite than host. He needs the dunces just as they need him. Without them, he could not, of course, turn satiric apology into satiric instance.

Despite, then, Pope's desire for, and efforts toward, absolute difference, he is finally and always already related to all those from whom he would distance and differentiate himself. The "trace" prevents both absolute difference and distinct identity, ensuring relation, for a "trace" of the "other" lies in the "same" and vice versa. The "trace," always "present" in writing, graphic or otherwise, is responsible for the play of difference that, in *Arbuthnot,* produces the relation, the mingling, and the intercourse that Pope would avoid.

9. The Vanity of Human Wishes:

A Conclusion in Which Nothing Is Concluded

The desire of a conclusion is as understandable as it is widespread. If we say such desire is natural, that may be revealing, for nature appears connected with our tendencies to mythologize or mythify. We naturally want (desire as well as lack) the comfort and solace afforded by a (fantasized) world in which conclusions are possible. As has been frequently suggested in the preceding chapters, however, such definiteness is impossible. In a recent essay entitled "Living On" Derrida has gone so far as to problematize even the seemingly indisputable opposition life/death.[1] The question of style is inescapable here. As I suggested earlier, the style of deconstruction is essayistic, precisely because, as Geoffrey Hartman remarks, the "consciously occasional nature of the essay prevents closure": "in an essayistic mode everything, including the ending, is always arbitrary or ironic: the one question dissolves into the many, and even the external as distinguished from the internal interruptions serve to keep things open."[2] Yet we continue to hope for, and expect, with Swift and Pope, straight lines, clear-cut choices, distinct identities, and absolute differences. (The reader will determine for himself or herself the relation of the tentative, the conventional, and the ironic in these hopeful con-cluding remarks.) Part of the immense potential and value of deconstruction lies in its Bible-like demonstration of the vanity of such human wishes.

To think about the vanity of human wishes, particularly after essays on Dryden, Swift, and Pope, is inevitably to call to mind Samuel Johnson, on whom the reader should logically expect a next essay in a more systematic account. Dr. Johnson wrote, of course, "The Vanity of Human Wishes" as well as the prose narrative *Rasselas,* both of which imitate the thought and spirit of the Book of Ecclesiastes. With some desire to suggest what might have been (and yet is), I invoke Johnson as a way of returning attention to Restoration and eighteenth-century texts. I hope that, along with some other recent writers, I have been able to advance the wedge slowly being driven into the mono-lithic—and essentially closed—scholarship on this crucial pe-riod in the history of English literature.

Generally we have imagined the Augustans either to be like us in their enlightenment or else totally other (for instance, quasi-medieval). But the certainties of our scholarship have begun to appear illusions, and Augustan texts now seem in-sightful to the extent that their own supposed certainties are rare. We may yet have much to learn from the Augustans, and if so deconstruction may be our route to that new old knowl-edge. So we can hope that further work will be done on Augus-tan texts, informed by deconstructive theory and practice.[3]

I hope, however, that if these essays have any impact, it will not be limited to Augustan studies. In addition—I hope—to shedding light on deconstruction and to inviting further work on Dryden, Swift, Pope, Johnson, and others, these essays enact, of course, a particular way of reading and pose some large questions about the ways we read and the responsibilities reading entails. Just as Derrida uses "writing" as a metaphor, so I regard "reading" as a powerful metaphor for a wide range of human activities. Deconstruction involves a particular way of seeing, and thus it has implications for the way we live. Indeed, the implications of certain themes recurring in this book are far-reaching. Not the least of these concerns difference, the desire of difference (an ambiguous enough phrase), and the dangers of difference. Further consideration of these matters should be fruitful, particularly if informed by not only the work of Derrida and other deconstructionists but also the recent efforts of René Girard and Bernard-Henri Lévy.[4] Of course, as indicated in my essay here on *An Epistle to Dr. Arbuthnot,* itself influenced by Girard's work, difference cannot be well considered apart from the issue of relation and relationality. One hardly has to be Nietzschean to understand the extent and depth of the biblical call to relation (rather than opposition or difference), and of course that biblical position is echoed in, among others, Marxism; consider for example, Robert Sayre's recent description of the Marxist position: "Men become what they become only together, in relationship to other men. The idea of the 'natural' individual existing at man's historical beginnings is a bourgeois myth of the eighteenth century."[5] Important common ground thus appears in perhaps unexpected places, and so the need is great for careful analysis of difference and relation in the Bible, Marxism, feminism (as the previous chapter should have suggested), and deconstruction—the rewards to be hoped for are also great. The same may be true in such Augustan writers as Pope, whose texts, we have begun to realize, offer valuable insight into that "enigmatic system of relatedness in which [man] is enclosed." If I may continue quoting Maynard Mack discussing *King Lear,* we may be able to grasp Pope's acknowledgment that man's fate "comes into being with his entry into relatedness, which is his entry into humanity."[6] In any case, deconstruction has implications well beyond the narrowly textual.

Despite what its opponents claim, then, deconstruction involves both a centrifugal and a centripetal movement. It moves both outward and inward, being neither simply Hellenistic nor

Hebraic in its direction. Such complications profoundly challenge our habitual ways of thinking, and they are unsettling to all of us, no matter how enlightened we believe ourselves to be. Like Yahweh, deconstruction acts as an agent of disillusionment, revealing the vanity of human wishes—and hopes.

The repeated hopes to which I have given expression in this (non)conclusion attest to the strength of illusion, the persistence of hope and vanity, and the nature of desire. "Ye who listen with credulity to the whispers of fancy, and pursue with eagerness the phantoms of hope; who expect that age will perform the promises of youth, and that the deficiencies of the present day will be supplied by the morrow. . . ."[7] Yet I believe the effects of deconstruction are demonstrated too, problematizing that congenial opening of *Rasselas*. Does not the Bible teach us, as deconstruction does, that hopelessness is as illusory as "the phantoms of hope"? Is not deconstruction, like the biblical "vision," a quest(ion)? "Henceforth, so that God may indeed be, as Jabès says, *an interrogation of God,* would we not have to transform a final affirmation into a question?"[8]

Notes

Introduction

1. See Derrida, *Positions,* trans. Alan Bass (Chicago: Univ. of Chicago Press, 1981); Terry Eagleton, *Walter Benjamin or Towards a Revolutionary Criticism* (London: Verso, 1981); Spivak and Ryan, "Anarchism Revisited: A New Philosophy," *Diacritics,* 8 (Summer 1978), 66-79; and Ryan, "New French Theory in *New German Critique,*" *New German Critique,* no. 22 (Winter 1981), 145–61. Michael Ryan's *Marxism and Deconstruction* (Baltimore: Johns Hopkins Univ. Press, 1982) appeared after the present manuscript was completed.

2. See, to cite but three of several possible titles, *Literature and Psychoanalysis: The Question of Reading: Otherwise,* ed. Shoshana Felman, nos. 55-56 of *Yale French Studies* (1977); *Psychoanalysis and the Question of the Text,* ed. Geoffrey Hartman, Selected Papers from the English Institute, 1976–77 (Baltimore: Johns Hopkins Univ. Press, 1978); and *The Literary Freud: Mechanisms of Defense and the Poetic Will,* ed. Joseph H. Smith, vol. 4 of *Psychiatry and the Humanities* (New Haven: Yale Univ. Press, 1980).

3. See Handelman, *The Slayers of Moses: The Emergence of Rabbinic Interpretation in Modern Literary Theory* (Albany: State Univ. of New York Press, 1982) and Lévy, *The Testament of God,* trans. George Holoch (New York: Harper and Row, 1980).

4. I refer in the notes below to chapters 1 and 2 to several studies bearing on this relation.

5. An introduction to deconstruction by Christopher Norris, *Deconstruction: Theory and Practice* (London: Methuen, 1982), which I review in a forthcoming issue of *MLN,* differs considerably from my effort here. More systematic than essayistic, Norris's book, among other things, attempts an "objective" assessment of deconstruction and does not therefore provide deconstructive readings as in part an illustration of deconstruction. Since I added this note, two other books on deconstruction have appeared: Jonathan Culler, *On Deconstruction: Theory and Criticism after Structuralism* (Ithaca: Cornell Univ. Press, 1982), and Vincent B. Leitch, *Deconstructive Criticism: An Advanced Introduction* (New York: Columbia Univ. Press, 1983).

6. See Hartman, *Saving the Text: Literature/Derrida/Philosophy* (Baltimore: Johns Hopkins Univ. Press, 1981).

7. William E. Cain, *College English,* 41 (1979), 367-82. I have responded to Cain in *College English,* 43 (1980), 304-5, partly reproduced here.

8. Cain, p. 381.

9. See, for example, Paul A. Bové, *Destructive Poetics: Heidegger and Modern American Poetry* (New York: Columbia Univ. Press, 1980), as well as various essays by William V. Spanos and others associated with the journal *boundary 2.*

10. Warner, *Reading "Clarissa"* (New Haven: Yale Univ. Press, 1979); de Man, "The Epistemology of Metaphor," *Critical Inquiry,* 5 (1978), 13-30.

11. Vincent B. Leitch, "The Lateral Dance: The Deconstructive Criticism of J. Hillis Miller," *Critical Inquiry,* 6 (1980), 599.

12. Miller, "The Critic as Host," in *Deconstruction and Criticism* (New York: Seabury Press, 1979), p. 222.

13. Derrida, *Of Grammatology,* trans. Gayatri Chakravorty Spivak (Baltimore: Johns Hopkins Univ. Press, 1976), p. 158.

14. See de Man, *Allegories of Reading: Figural Language in Rousseau, Nietzsche, Rilke, and Proust* (New Haven: Yale Univ. Press, 1979), p. ix, and "Introduction" to a special issue of *Studies in Romanticism,* 18 (1979), 498. For de Man a deconstructive reading consists, first of all, in showing how a text's figural language deconstructs its thematic totalizations.

15. See Levin, *New Readings vs. Old Plays: Recent Trends in the Reinterpretation of English Renaissance Drama* (Chicago: Univ. of Chicago Press, 1979).

16. Spivak, "Translator's Preface," *Of Grammatology,* p. xlix; see also p. lxxvii.

17. Davis, *The Act of Interpretation: A Critique of Literary Reason* (Chicago: Univ. of Chicago Press, 1978), p. 2.

18. Ibid., p. 3.

19. Michael Hancher, "Understanding Poetic Speech Acts," *College English,* 36 (1974), 632.

20. Miller, "The Critic as Host," p. 224.

Chapter 1

1. Ferdinand de Saussure, *Course in General Linguistics,* trans. Wade Baskin (New York: McGraw-Hill, 1959), p. 67.

2. Ibid., p. 165.

3. Derrida, *Positions,* p. 27.

4. This paragraph and other points in this chapter are indebted to Alan Bass, "'Literature'/Literature," which appeared in *MLN* in 1972 and is reprinted in *Velocities of Change,* ed. Richard Macksey (Baltimore: Johns Hopkins Univ. Press, 1974). See, especially, pp. 344-45 of the reprinting.

5. Derrida, "Differance," in *Speech and Phenomena and Other Essays on Husserl's Theory of Signs,* trans. David B. Allison (Evanston, Ill.: Northwestern Univ. Press, 1973), pp. 142–43.

6. Introductory note to Derrida's "Freud and the Scene of Writing," which Mehlman translated for his collection *French Freud, Yale French Studies,* 48 (1973), 73.

7. Spivak, "Translator's Preface," *Of Grammatology,* p. xvii.

8. Derrida, *Of Grammatology,* pp. 62-63.

9. Bass, " 'Literature'/Literature," p. 345.

10. Derrida, *Of Grammatology,* p. 19.

11. Ibid., p. 143.

12. Derrida, *Positions,* p. 41.

13. Derrida, "Structure, Sign, and Play in the Discourse of the Human Sciences," in *The Structuralist Controversy: The Languages of Criticism and the Sciences of Man,* ed. Richard Macksey and Eugenio Donato (Baltimore: Johns Hopkins Univ. Press, 1972), p. 256. Cf. the description of deconstruction offered by Eugene Goodheart: "Unlike demystification, deconstruction is an assault on stable hierarchical notions of reality. To demystify is to reduce *a* to *b* or to evaporate illusion *a* in favor of reality *b.* Deconstruction, on the other hand, ambiguously preserves everything and makes everything the object of suspicion. Nothing disappears, but nothing is stable" (*The Failure of Criticism,* Cambridge, Mass.: Harvard Univ. Press, 1978, p. 3).

14. Spivak, "Translator's Preface," p. xviii.

15. See, esp., *Dissemination,* trans. Barbara Johnson (Chicago: Univ. of Chicago Press, 1981), and "White Mythology," trans. F. C. T. Moore, *New Literary History,* 6 (1974), 1-73.

16. In this paragraph I draw upon and quote Bass, " 'Literature'/Literature," pp. 347-48.

17. Johnson, "Translator's Introduction," *Dissemination,* p. xiii.

18. Ibid.

19. Derrida, "Structure, Sign, and Play in the Discourse of the Human Sciences," p. 249.

20. Bass, " 'Literature'/Literature," p. 349.

21. Derrida, *Of Grammatology,* p. 65.

22. Bass, " 'Literature'/Literature," p. 350.

23. Spivak, "Translator's Preface," p. xlix. Here, and elsewhere, I am deeply indebted to Spivak.

24. Ibid., p. xlvi. The Freudian passage is quoted on this page.

25. Derrida, *Of Grammatology,* p. 158.

26. "The Deconstructive Angel" appeared in *Critical Inquiry,* 4 (1977), 426-38. Miller's review was "Tradition and Difference," *Diacritics,* 2 (Winter 1972), 6-13.

27. Miller, *Thomas Hardy: Distance and Desire* (Cambridge: Belknap Press of Harvard Univ. Press, 1970), p. ix.

28. Spivak, "Translator's Preface," p. lxxv, and *Of Grammatology,* p. 158.

29. Miller, *Poets of Reality: Six Twentieth-Century Writers* (1965; rpt. New York: Atheneum, 1974), p. 3.

30. Herbert N. Schneidau, *Sacred Discontent: The Bible and Western Tradition* (Baton Rouge: Louisiana State Univ. Press, 1976).

31. Miller, "Tradition and Difference," pp. 6, 12.

32. Nietzsche, *The Will to Power,* ed. Walter Kaufmann, trans. Walter Kaufmann and R. J. Hollingdale (New York: Vintage Books, 1968), pp. 323, 327, 342. Miller cites these passages in "Tradition and Difference."

33. I draw on and quote Spivak, "Translator's Preface," pp. lxxvii-lxxviii.

34. Derrida, "Structure, Sign, and Play in the Discourse of the Human Sciences," pp. 264-65.

35. Schneidau, p. 180.

36. Ibid., pp. 48-49.

37. Derrida, "Differance," in *Speech and Phenomena,* p. 134.

38. See, esp., Thomas J. J. Altizer, *Total Presence: The Language of Jesus and the Language of Today* (New York: Seabury Press, 1980); *Deconstruction and Theology,* by Altizer et al. (New York: Continuum, 1982), which appeared after my manuscript was completed; John Dominic Crossan, *The Dark Interval: Towards a Theology of Story* (Niles, Ill.: Argus Press, 1975), *Raid on the Articulate: Comic Eschatology in Jesus and Borges* (New York: Harper and Row, 1976), and *Cliffs of Fall: Paradox and Polyvalence in the Parables of Jesus* (New York: Seabury Press, 1980); Robert Detweiler, *Story, Sign, and Self: Phenomenology and Structuralism as Literary-Critical Methods* (Philadelphia: Fortress Press, and Missoula, Mont.: Scholars Press, 1978); and Andrew J. McKenna's review of Crossan's 1976 book, "Biblioclasm: Joycing Jesus and Borges," *Diacritics,* 8 (Fall 1978), 15-29.

Chapter 2

1. Gerald Graff, "Fear and Trembling at Yale," *American Scholar,* 46 (1977), 477. Though he is almost always included in the "Yale School," Bloom is not, in my view, a deconstructionist. Despite important differences, Hartman does, I think, belong (uneasily and problematically) in any account of deconstruction.

2. Ibid., p. 478.

3. Quoted in ibid., pp. 472-73. The Derridean text is "Structure, Sign, and Play in the Discourse of the Human Sciences," which Graff cites from *The Structuralist Controversy,* ed. Macksey and Donato, p. 264.

4. Graff, "Fear and Trembling at Yale," p. 473.

5. See, for example, Geoffrey Hartman, *Criticism in the Wilderness: The Study of Literature Today* (New Haven: Yale Univ. Press, 1980), p. 239. The essay from which I quote was originally published as "Literary Criticism and Its Discontents," *Critical Inquiry,* 3 (1976), 203-20.

6. Jonathan Swift, *A Tale of a Tub,* in *"Gulliver's Travels" and Other Writings,* ed. Louis A. Landa (Boston: Houghton Mifflin, 1960), pp. 324-25. I develop the point in chapter 7 below.

7. Reinhold Niebuhr, *Faith and History: A Comparison of Christian and Modern Views of History* (New York: Scribner's, 1949), p. 16.

8. Hartman, *Criticism in the Wilderness,* pp. 227, 226, 232.

9. Bass, " 'Literature'/Literature," p. 350. Cf. Jonathan Culler: "Interpretation is not a matter of recovering some meaning that lies behind the work and serves as a centre governing its structure; it is rather an attempt to participate in and observe the play of possible meanings to which the text gives access" (*Structuralist Poetics: Structuralism, Linguistics, and the Study of Literature,* Ithaca, N.Y.: Cornell Univ. Press, 1975, p. 247).

10. Hartman, *Criticism in the Wilderness,* p. 257. The essay from which I quote was originally published as "The Recognition Scene of Criticism," *Critical Inquiry,* 4 (1977), 407-16.

11. Hartman, *Criticism in the Wilderness,* p. 256.

12. Ibid., p. 233.

13. Hartman, *Saving the Text,* p. 18. The essay from which I quote was originally published as "Monsieur Texte: On Jacques Derrida, His *Glas,*" *Georgia Review,* 29 (1975), 759-93.

14. Hartman, *Criticism in the Wilderness,* p. 206. The essay from which I quote was originally published as "Crossing Over: Literary Commentary as Literature," *Contemporary Literature,* 28 (1976), 257-76.

15. Bass, " 'Literature'/Literature," pp. 349-50.

16. Hartman, *The Fate of Reading and Other Essays* (Chicago: Univ. of Chicago Press, 1975), pp. 18, 19.

17. Derrida, *Of Grammatology,* p. 18.

18. Roland Barthes, "L'analyse structural du récit: à propos d'Actes X-XI," in *Exégèse et herméneutique,* ed. Xavier Léon-Dufour (Paris: Seuil, 1971), p. 200.

19. Hartman, *Criticism in the Wilderness,* p. 205. Of course, difference remains for Derrida. Difference *within* does mitigate difference *between,* however.

20. Hartman, *The Fate of Reading,* p. 13.

21. Leslie Dewart, *The Future of Belief* (New York: Herder and Herder, 1966), p. 120.

22. Thomas J. J. Altizer, *The Gospel of Christian Atheism* (Philadelphia: Westminster, 1966), p. 42.

23. Ibid., p. 149. I am not sure that Nietzsche thought there ever was an "original center."

24. Crossan, *Raid on the Articulate,* p. 44.

25. Crossan, *The Dark Interval,* p. 43. For more recent work by Crossan, as well as Altizer, see above, chapter 1, note 38.

26. Harvey Cox, *On Not Leaving It to the Snake* (New York: Macmillan, 1967), p. 38.

27. Schneidau, *Sacred Discontent,* p. 259.

28. Harold Bloom, *A Map of Misreading* (New York: Oxford Univ. Press, 1975), pp. 42-43. For further discussion of these and related points, see Handelman, *The Slayers of Moses,* which appeared after my manuscript was completed.

29. Thorleif Boman, *Hebrew Thought Compared with Greek,* trans. Jules L. Moreau (London: SCM Press, 1960), p. 68.

30. Ibid., p. 151.

31. Bloom, *A Map of Misreading,* p. 43.

32. Hartman, *Saving the Text,* p. 18.

33. Hartman, *The Unmediated Vision* (1954; rpt. New York: Harcourt, Brace, 1966), p. 173.

34. Derrida, *Writing and Difference,* trans. Alan Bass (Chicago: Univ. of Chicago Press, 1978), p. 82. The quotation from *Culture and Anarchy* appears on p. 79.

35. Ibid., p. 64. See also the discussion of Jabès in the chapter entitled "Ellipsis."

36. Ibid., p. 65.

37. Schneidau, *Sacred Discontent,* p. 99 n.

38. Crossan, *Raid on the Articulate,* pp. 149, 174.

39. Hartman, *The Fate of Reading,* p. 309.

40. Cox, *On Not Leaving It to the Snake,* p. 11.

41. Ibid., p. 114. The second quotation is by Dewart as cited in Cox, p. 81. Of course, as Cox suggests, that being made will be a re-creation, beginnings having always already begun, and not absolutely different.

42. Altizer, *The Gospel of Christian Atheism,* p. 151.

43. Nietzsche, *The Will to Power,* p. 98.

44. McKenna, "Biblioclasm," p. 27.

45. See ibid., p. 22.

46. Ibid., p. 29.

47. Derrida, "Differance," pp. 134-35.

Chapter 3

1. See also the review essay focusing on *Criticism in the Wilderness* by Kenneth Johnston in *College English,* 43 (1981), 471–89.

2. Geoffrey Hartman's term; see *Criticism in the Wilderness,* p. 226. Subsequent references to this book will be cited as *CW* and given in the text.

3. Jane P. Tompkins, "The Reader in History," in her edition of *Reader-Response Criticism* (Baltimore: Johns Hopkins Univ. Press, 1980), p. 198.

4. Ibid., p. ix.

5. Steven J. Mailloux, "Learning to Read: Interpretation and Reader-Response Criticism," *Studies in the Literary Imagination,* 12 (1979), 93-108.

6. Ibid., p. 95.

7. Ibid.

8. Hartman, *Saving the Text,* pp. 141-42. Subsequent references to this book will be cited as *STT* and given in the text.

9. Susan A. Handelman, review of *Criticism in the Wilderness,* in *Wordsworth Circle,* 12 (1981), 203.

10. Martin Buber, *I and Thou,* trans. Ronald G. Smith, 2nd ed. (New York: Scribner's, 1958), p. 126; John Shelby Spong, *This Hebrew Lord* (New York: Seabury Press, 1974), p. 70 and passim.

11. See Robert Con Davis, "Critical Introduction: The Discourse of the Father," in his collection *The Fictional Father: Lacanian Readings of the Text* (Amherst: Univ. of Massachusetts Press, 1981), pp. 1-26.

12. Harold Bloom, *Kabbalah and Criticism* (New York: Seabury Press, 1975), p. 82.

13. Handelman, "Freud's Midrash: The Exile of Interpretation," in *Intertextuality,* ed. Jeanine Parisier Plottel and Hanna Charney (New York: New York Literary Forum, 1978), p. 107. This essay is reprinted in her *Slayers of Moses.*

14. Handelman, "Freud's Midrash," p. 102.

15. Ibid., p. 109.

Chapter 4

1. See, for example, The Christian Critic Series volume *Gerard Manley Hopkins,* ed. James F. and Carolyn D. Scott (St. Louis: B. Herder, n.d.), which reprints "The Creation of the Self in Gerard Manley Hopkins" from *ELH,* 22 (1955), 293–319, and *Religion and Modern Literature: Essays in Theory and Criticism,* ed. G. B. Tennyson and Edward E. Ericson, Jr. (Grand Rapids, Mich.: Eerdmans, 1975), which reprints "Literature and Religion" (see note 2 below).

2. Miller, "Literature and Religion," in *Relations of Literary Study,* ed. James E. Thorpe (New York: Modern Language Association, 1968), p. 125. See also Robert Moynihan, "Interview with J. Hillis Miller, Yale, Fall, 1979," *Criticism,* 24 (1982), 99-125.

3. Harold Fromm, "Sparrows and Scholars: Literary Criticism and the Sanctification of Data," *Georgia Review,* 33 (1979), 262, 269-70. See also Graff, "Fear and Trembling at Yale," pp. 467-78.

4. Fromm, "Sparrows and Scholars," p. 275.

5. See Sarah Lawall, *Critics of Consciousness: The Existential Structures of Literature* (Cambridge, Mass.: Harvard Univ. Press, 1968), Vernon Ruland, *Horizons of Criticism: An Assessment of Religious-Literary Options* (Chicago: American Library Association, 1975), and Vincent B. Leitch, "A Primer of Recent Critical Theories," *College English,* 39 (1977), 138-52. See also Susan Hawkins Miller, "The Endless Calculus of Critical Language," *Denver Quarterly,* 16 (Winter 1982), 57-74.

6. Miller, *The Disappearance of God: Five Nineteenth-Century Writers* (1963; rpt. Cambridge, Mass.: Belknap Press of Harvard Univ. Press, 1975), p. 312.

7. Ibid., p. 359; Lawall, *Critics of Consciousness,* p. 208.

8. Miller, *The Disappearance of God,* p. 359.

9. Miller, *Poets of Reality,* pp. 1, 3-4.

10. Ibid., pp. 7, 8.

11. Lawall, *Critics of Consciousness,* p. 202.

12. Miller, *Poets of Reality,* p. 312.

13. Ibid., pp. 123-24.

14. Ibid., p. 179.

15. Ibid., p. 358. A similar position appears in Miller's introduction to the Twentieth-Century Views volume on Williams, which he edited (Englewood Cliffs, N.J.: Prentice-Hall, 1966), pp. 1-14.

16. Miller, "Williams' *Spring and All* and the Progress of Poetry," *Daedalus,* 99 (1970), 417, 418, 419.

17. Ibid., p. 427.

18. Ibid., p. 429.

19. On this point, see Miller, "The Critic as Host."

20. Miller, "Williams' *Spring and All* and the Progress of Poetry," p. 429.

21. Ibid., pp. 429, 430.

22. Miller, "Georges Poulet's 'Criticism of Identification,' " in *The Quest for Imagination,* ed. O. B. Hardison, Jr. (Cleveland: Case Western Reserve Univ. Press, 1971), p. 210. Cf. Miller, "The Literary Criticism of Georges Poulet," *MLN,* 78 (1963), 471-88.

23. Miller, "Georges Poulet's 'Criticism of Identification,' " p. 216. I shall consider this passage at greater length in the next chapter.

24. Ibid., p. 217.

25. Miller, *The Disappearance of God,* p. vii.

26. Ibid., pp. xii-xiii.

27. Miller, *Charles Dickens: The World of His Novels* (1958; rpt. Bloomington: Indiana Univ. Press, 1973), p. 274.

28. Ibid., p. 333.

29. Ibid., p. 327.

30. Miller, *The Form of Victorian Fiction* (Notre Dame, Ind.: Univ. of Notre Dame Press, 1968), pp. 109-10. Cf. Miller's point in *Thomas Hardy,* p. 154, that "the only happy love relationship for Hardy is one which is not union but the lovers' acceptance of the gap between them."

31. Crossan, *The Dark Interval,* pp. 45-46.

32. Ibid., pp. 121-22.

33. Quoted in Crossan, *Raid on the Articulate,* pp. 39-40.

34. Ibid., p. 178.

35. Ibid., pp. 148, 73.

36. See in this regard Derrida's essays on Jabès and Levinas in *Writing and Difference.*

37. Miller, "Tradition and Difference," p. 11. See, esp., Schneidau's chapter "In Praise of Alienation" in *Sacred Discontent,* pp. 1-49.

Chapter 5

1. *Critical Inquiry,* 6 (1980), 593-607. I shall give page references to Leitch's essay, as well as Miller's response, in my text.

2. Miller, "The Critic as Host," pp. 217-53. This is an expanded version of an essay with the same title that appeared in *Critical Inquiry,* 3 (1977), 439-47.

3. Cain, "Deconstruction in America: The Recent Literary Criticism of J. Hillis Miller."

4. "Theory" derives from the Greek *theoria:* a "looking at." Thus deconstruction, which seeks only to question, wonder, and look at, without ever expecting to arrive at "the truth," deserves the epithet "theoretical." I owe this point and others to my former student Christopher Ryan, who has taught me much.

5. Miller, "The Critic as Host," p. 224.

6. Miller, "Georges Poulet's 'Criticism of Identification,' " p. 216.

7. Leitch claims, however, that "the rift between Poulet and Derrida dramatizes the either/or choice presented in the 1971 essay" (p. 594). But see Miller's point in the Preface added to the reprinting of *The Disappearance of God* (1963; rpt. 1975): "It appears that the relation between my present work and that of over a decade ago is more than simply negative" (p. xii).

8. De Man, *Allegories of Reading,* p. 245.

9. Cf. Miller's "On Edge: The Crossways of Contemporary Criticism," *Bulletin of the American Academy of Arts and Sciences,* 32 (Jan. 1979), 17: "The range of viable alternatives in literary methodology has become bafflingly large. These alternatives can, so it seems, hardly be reconciled in some grand synthesis. *Il faut choisir.* "

10. See also ibid., pp. 13-32.

11. Cain, "Deconstruction in America," p. 381.

12. Derrida, *Positions,* p. 42. Various other texts might be cited here, but see especially *Spurs: Nietzsche's Styles,* trans. Barbara Harlow (Chicago: Univ. of Chicago Press, 1979), p. 81.

13. Miller, "Stevens' Rock and Criticism as Cure, II," *Georgia Review,* 30 (1976), 330-48.

14. The point is that which Miller also makes in the new Preface written for the 1975 reprinting of *The Disappearance of God* (pp. xii-xiii), which I quoted in the previous chapter.

15. Miller, "Williams' *Spring and All* and the Progress of Poetry," p. 430.

16. Cain has noted a number of "contradictions" in Miller's texts but has not read the allegory in/of these texts.

17. Miller, "Ariachne's Broken Woof," *Georgia Review,* 31 (1977), 59-60.

18. De Man, *Allegories of Reading,* p. 242.

Chapter 6

1. *The Faith of John Dryden: Change and Continuity* (Lexington: Univ. Press of Kentucky, 1980). See also my essay "Dryden's *Religio Laici:* A Reappraisal," *Studies in Philology,* 75 (1978), 347-70.

2. The text used throughout is *The Works of John Dryden,* ed. E. N. Hooker, H. T. Swedenberg, Jr., et al., II (*Poems, 1681-1684,* ed. H. T. Swedenberg, Jr.) (Berkeley: Univ. of California Press, 1956–). I identify the poem by line number, the prose Preface by page number in this edition.

3. I quote the commendatory verses, here and below, from the second volume of *The Works of John Dryden,* cited above.

4. *The Several Ways of Resolving Faith By the Controvertists of the Roman and Reformed Religion,* 2d ed. (London, 1682), pp. 59-60; quoted in *The Faith of John Dryden,* p. 91.

5. I quote Stanley Fish's description of his 1980 NEH Summer Seminar on "Milton and the Fall into Reading."

6. Tillotson, *The Rule of Faith: or an Answer to the Treatise of Mr. I. S. entituled, Sure-footing, Etc.* (London, 1676), p. 106; Care, *Utrum Horum: or, The Nine and Thirty Articles of the Church of England, At large recited* . . . (London, 1682), p. 17; quoted in *The Faith of John Dryden,* p. 90.

7. See, esp., pp. 91-95.

8. See Johnson, "Translator's Introduction," *Dissemination,* p. xi, and Derrida, *Of Grammatology,* p. 143.

9. De Man, *Allegories of Reading,* p. 9.

10. Ibid., p. 12.

11. Ibid.

12. See Nietzsche, *The Anti-Christ,* no. 32, and McKenna, "Biblioclasm," pp. 15-29.

Chapter 7

1. The text of *A Tale of a Tub* used throughout is *"Gulliver's Travels" and Other Writings,* ed. Louis A. Landa (Boston: Houghton Mifflin, 1960), with page references given in my text.

2. I have discussed this issue, in somewhat similar but briefer terms, in "Interpretation and Meaning in *A Tale of a Tub,*" *Essays in Literature,* 8 (1981), 233-39. I have found the following studies particularly useful in threading my way through the maze of Swift's text: Ronald Paulson, *Theme and Structure in Swift's "A Tale of a Tub"* (New Haven: Yale Univ. Press, 1960), and John R. Clark, *Form and Frenzy in "A Tale of a Tub"* (Ithaca: Cornell Univ. Press, 1969).

3. See Miller, "Georges Poulet's 'Criticism of Identification,' " pp. 191-224, and "Tradition and Difference," pp. 6-13.

4. Hartman, *Saving the Text.*

5. See, in this connection, Barbara Johnson, *The Critical Difference: Essays in the Contemporary Rhetoric of Reading* (Baltimore: Johns Hopkins Univ. Press, 1980).

6. Hartman's term; see *Criticism in the Wilderness,* p. 226.

7. See de Man's *Blindness and Insight: Essays in the Rhetoric of Contemporary Criticism* (New York: Oxford Univ. Press, 1971).

8. See the unpublished essay by my former student Michael Kilduff entitled "Satire of Reading: Swift's *A Tale of a Tub.*"

9. On this point, as well as others relating to the *Tale,* see Maureen Quilligan, *The Language of Allegory: Defining the Genre* (Ithaca: Cornell Univ. Press, 1979).

10. Johnson, "Translator's Introduction," *Dissemination,* p. ix.

11. Derrida, *Of Grammatology,* p. 143.

12. See also Quilligan, *The Language of Allegory,* pp. 66-67, for such wordplay as that on "textus" as both coat and text.

13. Swift does attempt to limit his points in the passage quoted to "such writers" as "the true illuminated." I argue that the issue is not the degree of authorial "sense" and control but language itself.

14. Johnson, "Translator's Introduction," *Dissemination,* p. xv.

Chapter 8

1. The text of Pope used throughout is the fourth volume of the Twickenham Edition of *The Poems of Alexander Pope: Imitations of Horace,* ed. John

Butt, 2nd ed. (New Haven: Yale Univ. Press, 1969); in quoting the "Advertisement" I reverse italics and Roman. Pope's admission that he wrote *Arbuthnot* "by snatches" has not deterred critics from arguing that the poem is a unity. See, for example, Elder Olson, "Rhetoric and the Appreciation of Pope," *Modern Philology,* 37 (1939–40), 13-35, and Elias F. Mengel, Jr., "Patterns of Imagery in Pope's *Arbuthnot,*" *PMLA,* 69 (1954), 184-97.

2. *The Works of Sir William Temple* (London, 1720), I, 289.

3. The point is made by, among many others, Dryden; see *"Of Dramatic Poesy" and Other Critical Essays,* ed. George Watson (New York. Dutton, 1962), II, 138.

4. Here, and throughout this paragraph, I draw on the important discussion by Peter Dixon, *The World of Pope's Satires* (London: Methuen, 1968).

5. Margaret W. Ferguson, "Border Territories of Defense: Freud and Defenses of Poetry," in *The Literary Freud: Mechanisms of Defense and the Poetic Will,* pp. 149-80. The quoted passages are from pp. 153, 155, and 159.

6. J. Paul Hunter, "Satiric Apology as Satiric Instance: Pope's *Arbuthnot,*" *Journal of English and Germanic Philology,* 68 (1969), 625-47.

7. René Girard, "The Plague in Literature and Myth," in his *"To Double Business Bound"* (Baltimore: Johns Hopkins Univ. Press, 1978), p. 138.

8. From "Inhibitions, Symptoms and Anxiety," quoted in Spivak, "Translator's Preface," *Of Grammatology,* p. xlvii. That the penis was represented as a quill in Pope's time is indicated in, for example, *Sawney and Colley (1742), and Other Pope Pamphlets,* ed. W. Powell Jones. The Augustan Reprint Society, No. 83 (Los Angeles, 1960).

9. Thomas E. Maresca, *Pope's Horatian Poems* (Columbus: Ohio State Univ. Press, 1966), p. 71. For other psychological readings of the Sporus passage, see Dustin H. Griffin, *Alexander Pope: The Poet in the Poems* (Princeton: Princeton Univ. Press, 1978), pp. 172-90, and John Trimble, "The Psychological Landscape of Pope's Life and Art," Diss. California-Berkeley 1971.

10. Williams, ed., *Poetry and Prose of Alexander Pope* (Boston: Houghton Mifflin, 1969), p. 207 n.

11. Miller, "The Critic as Host," p. 221.

12. Ibid.

Chapter 9

1. Jacques Derrida, "Living On: Border Lines," trans. James Hulbert, in *Deconstruction and Criticism,* pp. 75-176.

2. Hartman, *Criticism in the Wilderness,* p. 193.

3. To such texts, I hope we can begin to understand, a both/and perspective should be brought. Consider the case of Pope, for instance. Rather than

a clear choice between competing "approaches" or methodologies, Pope's poetry itself requires what I call reader-responsibility criticism, and that involves at least three (related) phases: (1) traditional-formalist, attending to what Walter A. Davis calls the immanent purposive movement of the text; (2) performative-response, which attends to both the dramatic act the poetry performs and the ways the reader is drawn in and directly involved; and (3) the deconstructive, attending to the differential play of language, which inevitably subverts the text's declarations. With Pope, at least, deconstruction, so often accused of licentious irresponsibility, emerges as an aspect or phase of responsible criticism. See Davis, *The Act of Interpretation;* in addition to reader-response criticism, consider the authorial-performative model, indebted to the later Wittgenstein and persuasively argued by Charles Altieri, *Act and Quality: A Theory of Literary Meaning and Humanistic Understanding* (Amherst: Univ. of Massachusetts Press, 1981); and see my prolegomenon on a book on Pope, "Pope's Poetry and the Reader's Responsibilities," *College Literature,* 9 (1982), 83-96.

4. See Girard, *Violence and the Sacred,* trans. Patrick Gregory (Baltimore: Johns Hopkins Univ. Press, 1977), *"To Double Business Bound"* and *Des choses cachées depuis la fondation du monde* (Paris: Grasset, 1978); and Lévy, *The Testament of God.* See also Michel Serres, *The Parasite,* trans. Lawrence R. Schehr (Baltimore: Johns Hopkins Univ. Press, 1982).

5. Sayre, *Solitude in Society: A Sociological Study in French Literature* (Cambridge, Mass.: Harvard Univ. Press, 1978), p. 3.

6. Mack, *"King Lear" in Our Time* (Berkeley: Univ. of California Press, 1965), p. 37.

7. Samuel Johnson, *The History of Rasselas, Prince of Abyssinia,* ed. Gwin J. Kolb (Arlington Heights, Ill.: Harlan Davidson, 1962), p. 1.

8. Derrida, "Edmond Jabès and the Question of the Book," in *Writing and Difference,* p. 78.

Index